S0-AGU-165

THE GREAT BARRIER REEF

a guide to the islands and resorts

Darwin

NORTHERN
TERRITORY

Alice Springs

QUEENSLAND

THE GREAT BARRIER REEF

WESTERN AUSTRALIA

Brisbane

SOUTH
AUSTRALIA

NEW
SOUTH WALES

Perth

Adelaide

Sydney

Melbourne

VICTORIA

TASMANIA

Hobart

by arne and ruth werchick

Acknowledgement
Publications of:
Australian Tourist Commission
3550 Wilshire Blvd.,Suite 1740
Los Angeles, CA 90010-2480
telephone numbers:
(213) 380-6060
(800) 445-4400

Copyright © 1986 by Arne and Ruth Werchick.

All rights reserved. No part of this book
may be reproduced, in any form or by any means,
without permission in writing from the publisher.

Printed in the United States of America

Published by Wide World Publishing/ Tetra
P.O. Box 476
San Carlos, CA 94070

CONTENTS

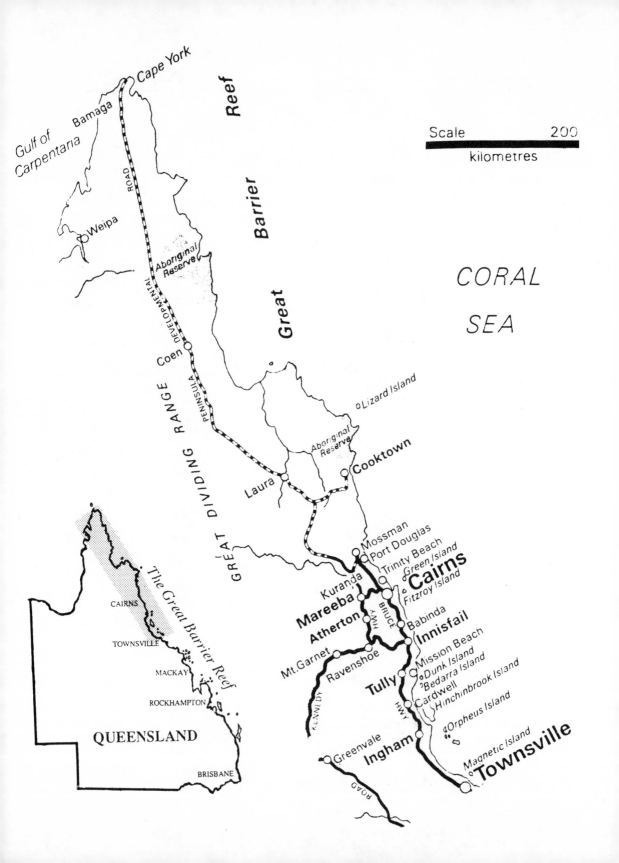

Cape York

Gulf of
Carpentaria

Bamaga

ROAD

Weipa

Aboriginal
Reserve

Coen

DEVELOPMENTAL

PENINSULA

GREAT DIVIDING RANGE

Laura

Reef

Barrier

Great

Lizard Island

Aboriginal
Reserve

Cooktown

CORAL

SEA

Scale   200

kilometres

Mossman
Port Douglas
Trinity Beach
Green Island
Cairns
Fitzroy Island

Kuranda

Mareeba

Atherton

BRUCE HWY

Babinda
Innisfail

Mt. Garnet

Ravenshoe

KENNEDY

Tully

Mission Beach
Dunk Island
Bedarra Island
Cardwell
Hinchinbrook Island

HWY

Greenvale

Ingham

Orpheus Island

Magnetic Island

Townsville

ROAD

CAIRNS

The Great Barrier Reef

TOWNSVILLE

MACKAY

ROCKHAMPTON

QUEENSLAND

BRISBANE

CONTENTS

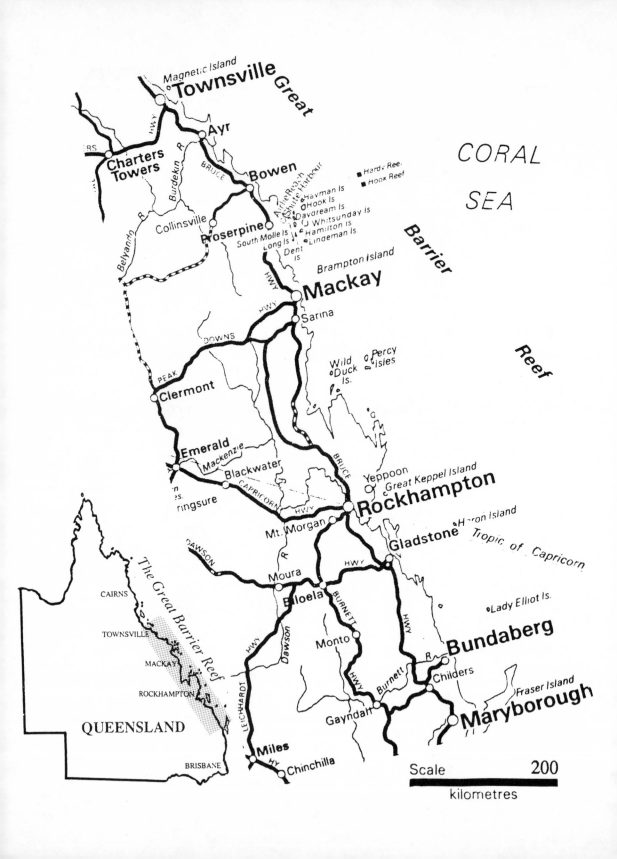

CONTENTS

sailing the Great Barrier Reef

In 1984 the Australian Tourist Commission, Qantas Airlines and the Queensland government, among others, intensified dramatically the campaign to bring more visitors to Australia. In the first three months of TV commercials in the U.S., over 100,000 Americans sought further information about travel *down under*. In 1984 during its first four months as an international jet gateway, Cairns, on Australia's northeast coast and adjacent to the Great Barrier Reef, was the point of entry for almost 9,000 American visitors.

We had visited Australia before and knew we would return to see more of the Barrier Reef – perhaps it was the advertising or just our happy memories of a comfortably superb, yet exciting vacation. Visiting Australia is like visiting with cousins with whom we have much in common, but who live in a place in so many respects quite different than ours. In any event, we just had to explore the Great Barrier Reef more fully.

Our plans first took us to a bookstore, then another and yet another, and finally to the Library of Congress index. We were astounded. There was no travel book which described the resort islands of the Great Barrier Reef in any detail, and precious little in print in the United States about the Reef at all. As we gathered travel brochures and government promotional literature from Australia, Queensland, the Whitsunday area, and other sources, we found that Australians themselves were unclear about many features of travel to North Queensland.

Depending upon whom we relied, for example, we found that Lindeman Island, a P. & O. resort in the Whitsunday Passage, was either 67 or 70 or 72 or 75 kilometers off the coast from Mackay. Not that the actual distance was that important. Since

sailing the Great Barrier Reef

the pilots with Lindeman Aerial Services and the captains of the giant catamaran ferries always hit the island right on the mark. But we were intrigued that descriptions of accommodations, prices, amenities and the like differed so.

Thus was born the idea for this book. It is as much a labor of affection for one of the truly magic places in the world, as a desire to try to fill a gap in travel information for the increasing thousands of Americans who will respond to the lure of this incredible marine holiday just as we have done.

> Arne & Ruth Werchick
> Sausalito, California

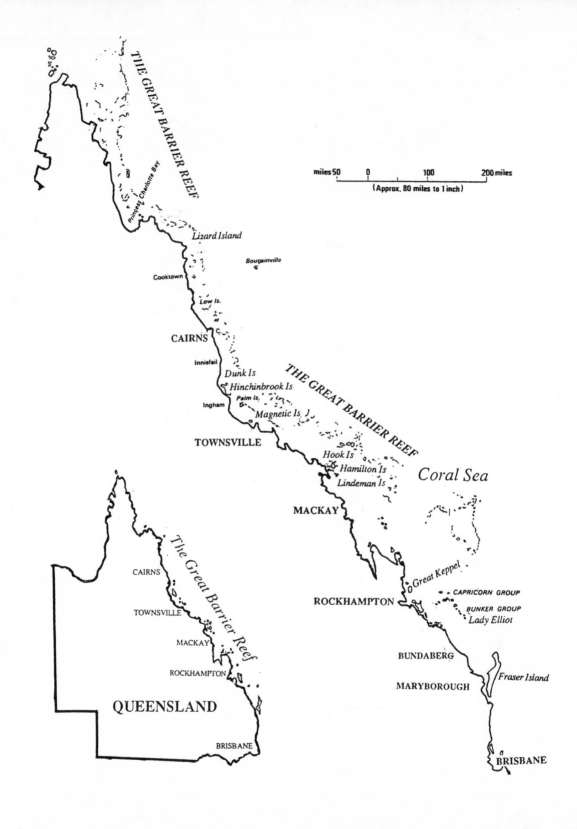

THE GREAT BARRIER REEF

Australia's Great Barrier Reef is without question one of the remaining natural wonders of the world and is without equal as a marine treasure.To see it, and particularly to walk upon it at low tide, gives a person an incredibly vivid sense of the power of the ocean and of the billions of coral polyps which over the ages make up a reef miles wide in places.To explore the islands, atolls and fringing reefs which owe their birth and continued existence to the protection of the the great Outer Reef with the ocean crashing against its sheer wall on the one side and with placid pools and lagoons inside this immense natural enclosure, imposes a sense of the vastness of the sea and its marine life, and a deep appreciation of the beauty of some of the oldest and the most varied forms of life on earth.

This huge living coral structure, occupying more than 72,000 square miles of ocean, extends from New Guinea in the Coral Sea southward to the Pacific Ocean below the fabled Tropic of Capricorn, which at 2327' latitude south of the equator marks the southern edge of the Torrid Zone. Some two thousand subordinate reefs – some developing over the past 15,000 years – are interspersed and often interlocked to make this continental barrier. These reefs grew as the sea level on the northeast continental shelf of Australia rose perhaps 150' over thousands of years to its present level, covering sites suitable for coral settlement and growth.

Glancing at a world map gives an idea of the tropical significance of this location. Rio de Janeiro lies near the Tropic of Capricorn. The northern equivalent of these latitudes – the tropic of Cancer at 2327' latitude north – incorporates Hawaii and the tropical Caribbean islands. These are the sunniest latitudes on earth.

The Outer Barrier Reef follows the coast of Queensland, Australia's huge northeastern state, for 1258 miles. The Australian Tourist Commission's very useful publication, *Destination Australia for 1984*, tells us it runs

> *from the very tip of Cape York Peninsula in the North of Queensland to below Gladstone in the south. Located 12 to 31 miles (20 to 50 km) offshore, the Reef acts as a barrier against the Pacific Ocean. The Outer Barrier Reef, an extensive coral platform, rises from the ocean floor; some sections are awash, others just beneath the waves. At low tide, parts of the oral mass are bared and you can explore the great coral grounds.*

The English explorer Captain James Cook, aboard the Endeavor in 1770, was the first European to discover this incredible reef – or at least the first to live to describe the voyage. The next European to pass through the region was Captain Bligh, in an open boat after the mutiny on the Bounty, en route from Tahiti to Timor in the Indian Ocean in May of 1789. Since the reefs discovery by Europeans, first navigators and later scientists, have puzzled over its origins and its immensity. Much is still unknown about this thousand mile wall running half the length of a continent just beneath the surface of the ocean. Just within the past year, a new deep water channel through the reef was discovered, cutting as much as a half day for freighters carrying commerce between Japan and Australia.

To the north, the Outer Reef is more a solid barrier with tortuous passages, some of them 50 miles long. As you move to the southern extremes, the Reef is much less continuous, more a succession of massive segments of reef – many several miles long and wide – with navigable channels. The lagoon filling the thousands of square miles between the Outer Reef and the mainland is literally a cornucopia of smaller coral reefs, coral cays and atolls and, near the coast, hundreds of continental and bush islands which the ages have gradually pulled from the mainland itself, and eons later provided with their own fringing reefs.

You can explore on foot (at low tide) and by snorkel and scuba diving many parts of the Great Barrier Reef itself and many of the abundant fringing reefs which have grown around the sheltered islands, and you will marvel at the variety of life ordinarily hidden beneath the sea. Almost all of the resorts in North Queensland offer excursions of one sort or another to the Outer Reef. These may be by boat or by air. Some resorts actually have barges moored permanently at the Outer Reef itself.

The Great Barrier Reef never contacts the mainland, and to see and appreciate it one must visit the varied and beautiful islands of the area. To do so not only offers the excitement of the Reef itself, but also promises one of the best tropical island vacations possible in the world–a vacation offering an exciting array of unique resorts, many set amidst national parks or naturally beautiful unspoiled surroundings.

The higher islands off the Queensland coast are generally

situated closer to the mainland. Most rise abruptly. Many of the islands within the protected waters of the Outer Reef are bordered by *fringing coral reefs,* within which thrive marine environments which are miniature versions of those within the Outer Reef itself. These subordinate reefs develop in shallower water rather close to the coasts of the high islands. They tend to be U-shaped because of the currents and winds. Depending upon the degree of protection, the weather conditions and other factors, some of these inner reefs are richer in coral and marine life than many portions of the Outer Reef itself and offer fantastic surface and underwater sightseeing opportunities.

In all, the Great Barrier Reef embraces nineteen developed islands with resort facilities, 2500 named reefs, 250 named continental islands, 71 named coral cays, and a total of more than 600 islands. All of the resort islands are leaseholds of government property, except Bedarra and Dunk, which became free holds through legislative anomaly early this century. Magnetic Island, not really a resort island in the true sense, but rather a suburban island with many motel and lodging facilities, is a considerably larger freehold island, parts of which later became converted to hotels and resorts. Most of the resort islands have also been classified in whole or in part as Australian national parks.

Many of these islands, with government approval, started as sheep stations or cattle ranches or other small business ventures and were later converted to resort facilities because, by quirk of Australian law, the leases were transferable. Yet today, because there were no early pastoral or other business leases on them, the large majority of Barrier Reef islands remain entirely and beautifully vacant.

THE GREAT BARRIER REEF

The Australian Great Barrier Reef Marine Park Act of 1975 established a region of over 17,000 square miles as protected area with plans ultimately to add the majority of the Barrier Reef to this Marine Park. For information about the Park, you can write to the Great Barrier Reef Marine Park Authority, P.O.Box 1379, Townsville, Qld.4810, Australia. In recognition of the unique significance of this natural treasure, the United Nations Education, Scientific and Cultural Organization in October 1981 added the Great Barrier Reef to the World Heritage List.

Hamilton Island

a colony of brain coral

Coral reefs are built over hundreds and thousands of years by microscopic living coral polyps, minute relatives of jellyfish and sea anemones. These remarkable tiny engineers ingest sea water, filter out nourishment, and from this *manufacture* calcium carbonate (limestone), which becomes their skeleton of hard coral. Different types of coral feed at different times of the day. While snorkeling or diving you can recognize feeding coral by the fact that it appears distinctly softer and fuzzier all over. Polyps that are not feeding will always appear to be smoother and harder.

Generation after coral generation is born, lives and dies atop one another. As they die, their infinitesimal *bones* interlock and pile on another to add to the bulk of a particular reef, and a new generation of colorful living coral replaces its ancestors. Coralline algae and other microscopic denizens of the ocean add to the structure and provide the organic cement which binds the reef together so firmly that after a point it becomes as hard as solid ground.

Coral reefs themselves become centers of sea life. Plants grow on and around them. Small and large sea creatures use them as sources of food, shelter from the sun, protection from predators. They wax and wane over the decades as the conditions of the sea change and as predatory forces attack or ignore them.

There are hundreds of different coral species. Dozens of species of soft corals do not have limestone skeletons and look like marine vegetation. The four hundred species of hard corals fall broadly into two main categories: *branching*, such as staghorn, needle, and knobby corals, and the beautiful ephemeral coral fans; or *rounded like boulders,* some of the most dramatic of which are the brain corals (almost perfectly round structures, from under six inches to huge bommies twenty-five or more feet in diameter, which actually appear to have convolutions like the human brain) or mushroom coral, sometimes called razor coral, large single polyp structures which have hundreds of individual razor-thin leaves like spokes around a center mouth.

Coral needs favorable conditions to survive and thrive. Until very recently, it was believed that water had to be shallow enough for abundant sunlight to penetrate in order to support coral polyps, which need plant life for oxygen and nutrition. Recent scientific research has uncovered algae which exist at depths previously thought impossible, living on the tiny fraction of sunlight which reaches the sea floor at eight hundred feet. Water *does* have to be salty, clear and warm (with average ocean temperature above 64° even in colder months). Most living reefs are less than 100 feet deep, although existence of reefs to depths more than 1/4 mile has been recognized, and this remains a scientific puzzle leading scholars to evolve theories of changing ocean depths over the centuries.

Coral reefs will not develop when they encounter fresh water, and thus even the Great Barrier Reef itself comes to an abrupt end off New Guinea where it encounters the muddy river waters flowing from the mountains of Papua. The cuts and channels which interrupt reefs, and the major sea channels which have been discovered to allow navigation across the Barrier Reef itself, mirror the variations in the flow and quality of the sea, sometimes reflecting river entrances on the adjacent coastline. Even the most perfect island reef must have at least one break to permit the lagoon to fill and empty with fresh sea water lest the entire inner fringing reef die.

Coral dies when exposed to the sun for more than a few hours.

While it produces heavy mucous secretions to protect itself from low tides and for brief exposure to the sun, prolonged exposure is fatal.Thus, if deprived of the nurturing sea for any length of time, areas of dead coral are left behind.

Living coral exists in a broad array of colors, but closer to the surface it seems to favor yellows, browns, greens and blues. Reds are less plentiful, and blacks are found generally at much greater depths. When coral dies it turns white, pale grey or dirty beige, with the exception of the deep water black coral and only a few of the red corals. All coral dies when removed from the sea. There is therefore no point to consider breaking the rules of the Barrier Reef by snapping off pieces of coral for a colorful souvenir. Aside from the fact that you will end up with a relatively nondescript piece of plain white coral, the powerfully unpleasant smell of the decaying polyps would be a reminder of your misdeed.

The Barrier Reef and its inner lagoons and fringing reefs is not the place for collecting corals and shells. There are numerous other island nations in the Pacific which have an abundance of marine life and do not currently object, vigorously, at any rate, to the taking of sea creatures as souvenirs. Australia, however, has good reason to want to protect the treasure of the Barrier Reef, and you will be reminded at each resort of the importance of leaving the Reef intact. Australian visitors, we might add, scrupulously respect this request and are almost unanimously careful about the health of their Reef.

As living coral reefs grow and grow over decades and centuries, they collect marine debris, including sand and pieces of seaborn broken coral.This leads to the formation of coral cays [generally pronounced *keys*], which gradually develop at the end of the

THE GREAT BARRIER REEF

reef away from the prevailing wind because of the action of wind, sun and sea. As this new *land* forms, the ocean and the wind, and perhaps bird life from nearby land, will later bring living seeds, leading to the development of the tropical vegetation commonly found on coral islands.

These cays are quite distinct from the islands usually found closer to the coast – the continental and bush islands – which are formed either by ancient volcanic activity or by having broken off from the coastline to which they were attached. Cays are commonly found immediately adjacent to the inner reefs and on the Outer Reef itself, but almost invariably at quite some distance from the mainland.

Coral reefs support an incredible array of marine flora and fauna. Here you may find sponges, shells, giant clams, sea cucumber (beche de mer, a delicacy in some oriental societies), benign starfish and the hideous and destructive Crown of Thorns starfish. If you look closely you can see six different species of giant sea turtles: *green, leatherback, flatback, loggerhead, hawksbill* and *Pacific Ridley*. All are protected by law. Even in shallower waters you will see more varieties of vividly colored tropical fish than you believed existed anywhere, ranging in size from a couple of inches to well over a foot. You will see or fish for sweetlip, emperors, snapper or coral trout, which may exceed two or even three feet in length. In deeper waters the Barrier Reef supports the largest marlin in the world, along with shark, sailfish, tuna and other exciting deep sea sport fish. In all, there have been 1500 species of fish identified in the Great Barrier Reef region.

Coral provides hours of fascination and delight. Unfortunately has a serious predator along the Great Barrier Reef. In the late

1960s scientists discovered that the population of a formerly obscure creature, the Crown of Thorns, a spiny dozen-legged starfish, had suddenly and inexplicably increased dramatically. This rather ugly echinoderm, which can grow to over a foot in diameter, feeds on living coral tissue leaving a trail of bleached white dead coral in its wake.

When the Crown of Thorns is less numerous, with just a few per acre, they feed at night digesting perhaps fifty square feet of coral a year – a limited assault which a healthy coral reef can usually tolerate. When their numbers reach the thousands on a segment of reef, however, these predatory starfish make short work of the reef, producing ninety percent destruction and leaving broad patches of permanently devastated reef. These predators, which may live for years, breed in midsummer when the female releases millions of eggs into the water. Fortunately, the mortality rate for this spawn is very high, but the potential for epidemic spread is always present.

For reasons still not clearly understood, the infestation of the '60s and '70s, which some doomsayers feared would devastate the entire length of the Great Barrier Reef before a solution could be found, retreated as mysteriously as it had begun. Is the danger passed? Many charter trip operators, particularly in the north, conduct periodic forays on their days off to keep the population of predators in their area of the Reef under control. Although we saw some Crown of Thorns, the government seems satisfied that the peril is history. Recently, however, *The Bulletin*, Australia's weekly news magazine affiliated with *Newsweek*, featured a cover story proclaiming that the plague has returned. Although there seems to be little general agreement with this frightening prediction, the Great Barrier Reef does remain vulnerable to this danger of devastation until scientists understand better what produces this massive invasion and how to deter it.

on Dunk Island

SEEING and DOING

Island holidays obviously conjure visions of sandy beaches, swimming in the ocean and in elegant resorts pools – perhaps with the tropical bar beside or in the middle for a bit of cool refreshment. Then there is plenty of rest and relaxation, and maybe golf or tennis, and of course a good restaurant here and there for relaxed dinners followed, perhaps with some music and a nice bar for a nightcap. The Great Barrier Reef of course provides ample doses of the classic island vacation, usually in the least crowed island resorts imaginable, but it offers, in addition, many experiences that few other areas of the world can match.

SNORKELING

Whether or not you have ever been much for water sports, or even if you are not a terribly strong swimmer, you will never forgive yourself if you visit the Barrier Reef without skin diving, or *snorkeling* , in these intensely blue translucent waters where underwater visibility fifteen or even twenty-five feet is not unusual. Snorkeling is named for its chief piece of equipment,the *snorkel,* which is nothing more than a rubberized tube with a mouthpiece, which you insert in your mouth while floating or swimming on the surface of the water.

This twelve to eighteen inch long tube is curved upward behind your head, so while you are staring with fascination at the coral and fish beneath you through a tempered glass face mask, you

25

are also breathing comfortably through the tube from the air above you. Your bathing costume is complete with the addition of a pair of swim fins which give you tremendous leg power in the water. Even if you could never tread water in a swimming pool, diving fins virtually allow you to stand upright in the ocean with your arms out of water, or to move forward swiftly with relaxed leg action.

Believe us: *snorkeling is very, very easy.* You don't have to dive into water with crashing waves or perform feats of strength or daring in the water to be good at this simple sport. At each resort, skilled and very cautious boat operators will take you out to quiet waters, show you how to snorkel, and then watch you to make sure you don't get into difficulty. Lots of snorkeling is done in waters shallow enough to stand upright, but do be careful not to stand on delicate coral and perhaps damage it permanently. The best snorkeling is also in calmer seas. Face it, fish prefer calm waters too. Fragile coral does not do particularly well in turbulent seas. In many instances at Heron Island or Hayman Island, for example, you can enjoy the sport by walking into the sea right off the beach at the edge of the resort and yet see thousands of beautiful fish and dozens of corals in shallow calm waters.

If we still have not soothed your deepest fears, you can go to a dive shop before your trip and take a brief snorkel lesson in their swimming pool. In fact such a stop, with or without the instructions, might be a wise idea. Although all of the resorts will lend or rent snorkel gear to you, one problem which you sometimes do encounter with snorkeling is finding equipment among the resort's supply which will fit you precisely.

When you get to the point where you love snorkeling so much that they have to drag you out of the water with a hook (which point we predict you will reach on your second day watching the fish), you will want swim fins and a face mask which fit as perfectly as possible. You may also want a mask which matches your vision correction if you wear glasses or contact lenses. We both wear contacts. One of us snorkels with lenses, while the other prefers the prescription face mask. For under $100 including the cost of the face mask, your dive shop can probably outfit you with a face mask fitted with a lens that is a very close approximation of most corrections for simple near or far-sightedness. Quality face masks with clear tempered glass will cost anywhere from $40 to over $100. By carrying your snorkel gear with you, you avoid the risk that the particular resort is out of your size or simply cannot give you a mask which keeps the water out of your eyes.

If you're still a little nervous about languidly swimming around a boat in water which might be deeper than you are tall, buy and bring one of the new light-weight belts which add a bit of support in the water. Even if you're very, very nervous about going in the water, do not give up hope; look into buying the least expensive available type of what divers call a buoyancy compensator or BC. This is nothing other than one of those inflatable life vests you have seen flight attendants on airlines demonstrate at the beginning of over-water flights. It fits over your head and straps around your waist. Blowing as much air into it as you need to be comfortable, you can float indefinitely on calm seas. It is the ultimate safeguard for the nervous snorkeler, but we predict that by the end of your first week you will wonder why you spent $75 for a BC.

THE GREAT BARRIER REEF

To find the best snorkeling in a particular area, look to where the coral thrives. There is little marine life of interest in areas where the reef has died.This means not too much prolonged exposure to direct sun at low tide and not too much crashing surf. Generally the best time for snorkeling is just after low tide on the incoming sea because the fish do not need to seek the protection of deeper water and shady crannies to escape the direct sun or low tide. The resort staff will gladly tell you how to find the best snorkeling.

Do remember that your back is exposed to the sun as you drift with the current, almost hypnotized by the teeming life just beneath the surface. A tee shirt or strong sun block, or both, should be part of the equipment of every snorkeler.

the joy of snorkeling

Many diving afficionados claim that the Great Barrier Reef offers some of the best natural conditions for scuba diving in the world. There are few wrecks to explore, but virtually everything else is there – plant and animal life, walls, caves, crevasses, deep coral formations, great photographic opportunities. All of this in an environment as safe for divers as anywhere in the world.

Several islands offer diving opportunities, and each resort claims to be the best. Heron, Lizard and Hayman Islands perhaps advertise diving more than the others, but nine other islands (Daydream,Great Keppel,Green, Fitzroy, Hamilton, Hinchin-brook, Long, Lady Elliot and South Molle) also offer at least some scuba diving opportunities. A few offer diving instruction packages.Tank refills are available at Daydream, Green, Hayman, Lady Elliot, Lizard, South Molle, and from the independent dive shop on Great Keppel. Most islands, however, currently do not have much in the way of rental equipment, and only a few offer specialized boating services to especially good tank dive spots in waters in the vicinity of the particular resort or to the Outer Reef. Hayman Island, for example, offers trips which will take divers to some highly regarded spots off the island and near adjacent Hook Island which offer excellent dive opportunities. Lizard Island has several outstanding dive spots within an hour's boat ride of the resort.

All resorts and charter boat operators indicate that they will definitely require that you have a regular valid diving certificate from one of the internationally recognized dive organizations such as PADI or NAUI or that you enroll in their diving program before they will furnish diving gear and services. In addition, some may expect you to bring your diving log. All of the resorts have masks and fins available for guests for use in snorkeling, but you may want to bring your own. Regulators are rather scarce, so you definitely should bring your own. Wet suits and buoyancy compensators can be rented on a few islands and not others. If you are travelling to different resorts and uninhabited islands, you will want to bring your own or call beforehand to check on availability.Tanks and weight belts are generally available.

on South Molle Island

MORE TO SEE AND DO

All of the resorts make available a wide variety of equipment for enjoying the water. At many islands, the use of this gear is included in your daily room rate, while at others varying charges are exacted for different activities. All of the resorts offer small sailing catamarans of the 11' to 14' variety and will happily show you how to enjoy them safely and comfortably in the bay right in front of the resort. There are pedal boats and even huge tricycles, on which two people can sit and pedal on top of the water. Windsurfers and paddle boards are seen everywhere. Most resorts also have small motor dinghies which you can take out for trips to nearby beaches.

Among other water sports found at Great Barrier Reef resorts, you will be offered paraflying, water skiing, trips in glass bottom boats, picnic excursions to adjacent islands, trips to underwater observatories and, of course, day and half-day fishing expeditions. Or there are small boats and jetties from which you may just drop a line and pull out a meal. All of the kitchens are happy to prepare your catch for your dinner.

Most of the resorts have fresh water swimming pools for your lounging and cooling off pleasure. At some, water volley ball is a popular sport. At others reading or enjoying a tropical drink are the busiest pool activities.

When you have absorbed enough water activity, you will find fascinating walking trails on most islands where you can see some of the most unusual bird and animal life outside of a zoo. On a few islands to the north, there are also rainforests which provide an exciting and perfectly safe walk through a tropical jungle.

Most resorts offer tennis courts (of widely varying quality) and

THE GREAT BARRIER REEF

a few have golf courses. Some have archery ranges.

This is a new style of island resorts on a group of uncrowded, generally unspoiled islands. There was little if any indigenous population on most of these islands for centuries, and there are only a couple of islands with any permanent residents aside from resort staff and the personnel attached to light houses or research stations. The resort islands are almost all surrounded by nearby, totally uninhabited islands for you to visit and explore, entirely by yourselves if you wish. The resort staff will leave you alone, and will return for you at whatever hour you specify. The only vehicles here are support and transport machines for the resorts. There are few roads and, when away from your hotel, no noises except the sea and the birds. There are few places in the world combining the opportunity for a vacation loaded with activity, yet rich in solitude and quiet.

on Dunk Island

Australia is very health and safety conscious. Food and water are extremely safe and pure. Airlines are as tightly regulated for safety as in the United States, if not more so. The captains who skipper your boats for islands tours are especially licensed, and those who sail you out to the Outer Barrier Reef itself are experienced and licensed with what are called *50 mile/ 50 ton* certificates.

Walking on the Reef is not always possible. Australians are safety conscious about such things and closely observe tide and weather conditions. To be sure that you will be able to actually walk on the Great Barrier Reef, you must allow time for tides and weather to be right.

There is little danger in the Barrier Reef area from plant or animal life. There is less shark danger to swimmers or divers in the waters off the resort islands than off the Pacific Coast of the United States. The sea bottom is relatively benign except for a few urchins and even fewer stone fish, which must not be stepped upon. There are a very few shell creatures – particularly the cone – which pack a very dangerous wallop if you pick them up. If you want to explore the sea bottom by hand, it is important to wear gloves and discuss the presence of any particular dangers with resort staff. When on an excursion near the Outer Reef, your skipper almost certainly will warn you against stepping on the Crown of Thorns starfish, which has hundreds of stickers which could inflict a nasty sting.

The only serious danger to swimmers and divers comes from the December to March invasion of venomous sea wasps, also known as box jelly fish. These translucent creatures, looking somewhat like an inverted floating plastic bag, have a box-shaped head about four to six inches across and are almost invisible without polaroid glasses. Their trailing tentacles, with hundreds of minute and poisonous stingers, can deliver a potentially fatal jolt to a human. These dangerous creatures breed in the inland waters, fortunately drift mainly near the surface and along the coast, and rarely are found near the islands or farther out toward the reef. They therefore have not constituted a serious problem on island resort beaches or in the deeper waters frequented by divers, and none of the island resorts has been menaced by them.

If there are any particular local perils, we have found the resorts and boat operators in the area to be very meticulous and conscientious about warning of even minimal risks.*We have listed the dangers here about which we were informed, but we encountered virtually none of them during our travels except for seeing a few Crown of Thorns and a very occasional, but quite visible sea urchin.*

One peril about which resorts do not warn adequately is the sun. You are very much in the tropics here, and the sun is exceptionally intense. Without protection the average person exposed to the midday sun (between 10:00 a.m. and 2:30 p.m.) will begin to burn in just 12 minutes! After 30 minutes you will experience appreciable discomfort; after one hour, peeling and blistering; and after two hours, possible permanent damage. Clouds give virtually no additional protection from the sun. Being on or near the water intensifies the risk because of reflected ultraviolet exposure. Even a suntan doesn't offer much real protection.

There are only two ways to minimize the risk of over-exposure to the sun: either stay out of the fun (*Stay out of the sun!* , you're saying, *but then why the devil did I fly 7500 miles*); or be smart and exercise great prudence by wearing hats and cover-ups, be aware of the time and intensity of your exposure to the sun, and *use protective lotions generously and regularly!* Now that sun lotions and creams are rated by protective power relative to how long they multiply natural resistance to sunburn, the choice is easier. We recommend regular use of sun blocks – that is, lotions or creams rated 15 or maximum protection – or their close relatives. And if you do get a sunburn, do stay out of the midday sun for at least a day or two. Don't worry; you'll soon build up that great tan even with this degree of sun protection, and your vacation won't be interrupted by the need to spend a week indoors writing postcards telling every one how much fun you were having.

One last precaution: during certain seasons and only on some islands, small biting insects – particularly what Australians call the sand fly, which is more like a flea – can be a terrible nuisance. Locals get used to them and are often unbothered. If you are hypersensitive or easily annoyed by these obnoxious creatures, remember to use any of the modern bug repellents liberally, especially around your feet and ankles. We found that every resort sold effective repellents, although we didn't see many creams or ointments designed exclusively to relieve the swelling and itch if you are attacked.

Bedarra Island

GET READY, GET SET

TRANSPORTATION

There are several airlines currently serving Australia from the United States, and there are several options available to get you to the Great Barrier Reef. Air fares are quite competitive for U.S. travel to this region, so the visitor has an interesting range of choices. We should also mention that Sydney's Kingsford Smith airport, with its separate international and domestic terminals, is efficient and an easy entry or departure point.

Pan American introduced non-stop overnight service from Los Angeles to Sydney using Boeing 747SP long-range planes and carried much of the traffic to Sydney and Melbourne with intermediate stops in Honolulu or Auckland as well. In recent years they placed great emphasis on their Clipper Class (or business class) service. In the Clipper class Pan Am uses what were formerly First Class seats and allows more leg room as well. We felt that the long trans-Pacific flight seemed to pass much more quickly and pleasantly in this class, and justified the additional expense to upgrade from economy fare. Because of the popularity of the mid-cabin (partly through the success of Pan Am's mileage bonus program in recent years) the aft section was sometimes less crowded, so even the passengers who paid lower fares found a bit of extra room for themselves.

In 1985 Pan Am set in motion the steps to turnover all of its Pacific routes, including Australia, to United Air Lines.

THE GREAT BARRIER REEF

United's plans for Australia have not been announced, other than to indicate that they will at least continue the service currently offered by Pan Am.

Continental Airline flies to Sydney via Honolulu as does CP Air (Canadian Pacific) and Qantas, Australia's own international air carrier. Qantas and UTA, the French long-distance carrier in the Pacific, also fly to Tahiti with service from Los Angeles to Papeete and on to Sydney. Qantas has recently added service from San Francisco and Los Angeles, (stopping in Honolulu, to Nadi, Fiji) which proceeds on to Sydney ,and intermediate service connecting Fiji and Cairns, Townsville or Brisbane.

If you wish to visit the Barrier Reef directly as the first or only destination on your journey, Qantas in 1984 introduced twice-a-week direct service connecting San Francisco, Los Angeles and Vancouver through Honolulu to Cairns, with on-going service to Brisbane and connections to Sydney and Melbourne. Using this very fine airline, it is also possible to visit other points in Australia. Qantas offers a circle fare allowing multiple stops on a round trip from the West Coast so long as you do not retrace your steps. You could therefore add stops in Brisbane, Sydney and Melbourne and see much of Australia for the same fare. Since Qantas serves New Guinea, it is also possible to add an exotic visit to Papua by including the Sydney-Port Moresby-Sydney service on this ticket, since Qantas does not serve New Guinea from any other gateway and therefore permits this retracing of steps on its circle fare.

One slight inconvenience which you must bear if you use the otherwise very convenient Qantas service rather than domestic carriers for internal flights in Australia is that, because it is exclusively an international carrier, each stop along the way is treated as an international flight with customs and immigration requirements even for transit passengers. This proved no great delay in Cairns or Brisbane during the trip we used Qantas, but we found ourselves in long lines at immigration at Sydney's Kingsford Smith airport.

Air New Zealand offers excellent regular DC-10 West Coast service to Australia via Aukland or Christ church and permits multiple stops en route on the same fare. The Australia cities included on this circle route are Melbourne, Sydney and Brisbane. By flying Air New Zealand, you could also add stops in Tahiti and Fiji. Because traffic is through Aukland, the airline obviously encourages you to include a visit to New Zealand. The airline staff is particularly congenial, the planes are sparkling clean, and the amenities were just about as nice as one can find in international travel. We found their service to be particularly prompt (with flights on a couple of legs actually departing a few minutes early because all reserved passengers had checked in), efficient and pleasant. Some travelers might want to see if Air New Zealand has changed their no-alcohol-served-on-Sunday rule before booking a Sunday flight.

Airline service all over the South Pacific is in the process of major changes and substantial growth, so you should work closely with a travel adviser as you prepare for your trip to see exactly what exciting combinations are available. Small regional airlines are expanding, and new international routes are being opened, particularly with the addition of new fuel-efficient jumbo jets to southern hemisphere airline fleets. Qantas, for example, has recently taken over management of Fiji's Air Pacific, which has routes from Honolulu to Nadi (pronounced *Nandi* in Fijian and, although not the capitol, is the international gateway to this nation of hundreds of islands), and Nadi to Brisbane, and they are looking for new airports to serve with Qantas' new Boeing 767s. Moreover, with the intense advertising campaign by both Australian and Queensland tourist commissions, it seems inevitable that more international air carriers will add direct routes to Cairns or Townsville which are vying for increased international air traffic.

Whether your holiday involves combining visits to several nations of the South Pacific, or a visit to all or just a part of Australia, the key to reaching the Barrier Reef by air will be getting to one of the gateway cities of Queensland: Cairns, Townsville, Prosperpine, Mackay, Rockhampton or Gladstone. From there the resort islands are reached by light aircraft connection or boat. With few exceptions, these resorts do not interconnect with each other by regular air, ferry or launch service, so visiting more than one resort will most often require going back to the coast.

Travel between major cities of Australia is via one of its two jet carriers, privately owned Ansett or government owned TAA (TransAustralia Airlines). There is a compact between these two carriers that they will operate the same routes at virtually the same times. This means that while TAA offered daily Sydney-Townsville service at 7:55 a.m., noon and 4:00 p.m., Ansett offered the same connection at 7:55 a.m., 11:50 a.m., and 4:15 p.m. Just about the only exception to this dual service is that currently Ansett is the exclusive jet air carrier to the new resort on Hamilton Island. Both carriers provide jet service to Cairns, Townsville, Proserpine, Mackay and Rockhampton. Service to Gladstone for Heron Island requires transfer to a regional or local carrier and is not by jet. The disadvantage of this service agreement to the traveller is a lack of competitive choices for times of departure. The advantage is that, should one carrier be fully booked, the other may have seats available.

While both companies provide friendly, safe and reasonably on-time service, there are some differences between TAA and Ansett. For shorter runs, Ansett operates principally with Boeing 737s while TAA uses chiefly DC9s (with a few 727s). The 737 seating is six across (three and three), while the DC9 is five across (three and two). For longer hauls, TAA uses Airbus A300s while Ansett has purchased Boeing 767s.

Occasionally the carriers will use different routes to the same destination. For example, on the day TAA flew from Sydney to Cairns (1228 miles direct) with a stop in Brisbane, Ansett offered service to Cairns with the stop in Townsville. The result was that the Ansett flight saved about a hundred miles and arrived almost two hours before the TAA service. It is worth checking (and re-checking after you arrive in Australia) to see exactly what service is available for the day you want to travel.

If you wish to change air carriers, Australian airlines don't automatically accept each other's tickets as most do airlines in the U.S. You must first go to the airline desk for the company on which you are ticketed and get an *endorsement* –which they will issue right there without any fuss – and then go to the counter of the company you want to fly with. While it takes only an extra minute to get the endorsement, at larger airports the TAA and Ansett desks are some distance apart – (in fact in separate buildings at Kingsford Smith airport in Sydney) it may take you fifteen or twenty minutes to get the tickets validated. It is wise, therefore, to allow extra time at the airport if you have switched airlines.

THE GREAT BARRIER REEF

The principal air terminals with jet service in North Queensland from north to south are Cairns and Townsville (which have international air service as well), Proserpine, Mackay and Rockhampton.

air distances between (miles) major cities

Cooktown – Cairns	107
Cairns – Townsville	177
Cairns – Brisbane	865
Cairns – Sydney	1228
Townsville – Proserpine	145
Townsville – Brisbane	692
Townsville – Sydney	1051
Proserpine – Mackay	63
Mackay – Rockhampton	174
Rockhampton – Gladstone	59
Gladstone – Brisbane	271
Brisbane – Sydney	450
Brisbane – Melbourne	857

Within Queensland, the principal air carrier is Air Queensland (the new name for BPA or Bush Pilots Airline, a colorful and accurately descriptive name which, in our estimation should not have been changed because they continue to be charmingly bush-league in several respects). Recently this carrier was acquired by TAA, although present plans are to continue separate operation. By a strange accident of fate, the line had contracted with TAA's competitor, Ansett, to use the Ansett computer system for its reservations operations, so for the next year a TAA company will be booking through Ansett's computers.

Omitting only a Cairns - Townsville route, and operating several familiar species of prop aircraft, Air Queensland connects all of the major cities and towns of Queensland, including service to Gladstone and Cooktown. Expansion plans call for purchase of a new generation of French jet-prop aircraft in the near future.

In addition, this carrier operates direct air service to several of the resorts: Brampton Island (daily from Mackay), Dunk Island (daily except Monday and Thursday from Cairns, and daily from Townsville), Hamilton Island (occasional service from Cairns, Mackay and Townsville), and Lizard Island (daily except Thursday from Cairns). Currently Air Queensland flights from Cairns may operate through TAA, or through Ansett, or through their own terminal at the general aviation airport which is over a mile to the north. Be sure to call and find out which terminal they're using for your flight, or you could end up carrying your luggage quite a way.

Air Whitsunday offers scheduled air service linking its home base, midway between Airlie Beach and Shute Harbor (just a few miles from Proserpine), with Mackay and Townsville. It also has scheduled seaplane service to Orpheus and Hinchinbrook Islands. In fact, because this plane stops at both islands, it is the only scheduled air link available between two Great Barrier Reef resorts without having to go back to the coast. Air Queensland has service from Lizard Island to Cairns, continuing on to Dunk Island; while a convenient connection, this does involve returning to a gateway city. Similarly, from Whitsunday Field, *Air Whit* also offers seaplane service to the resorts of the Whitsunday Group on a charter basis, and occasional scheduled flights as well, using 3-passenger Lake Buccaneers or 13-passenger Grumman Mallards, so there are through connections possible from Hinchinbrook and Orpheus to the Whitsunday Group.

Many small air services operate from the coast, serving various island resorts. For example, Lindeman Aerial Service from Mackay serves its namesake resort,and Hamilton Air Services operates helicopters for reef excursions and small planes for charter and regular service to Mackay and other gateways. Sunstate connects Rockhampton and Great Keppel Island with 15-minute flights, and Helitrans operates helicopter service to Heron Island out of Gladstone airport.

We concluded that there currently are insufficient practical boat connections from gateway cities to the Barrier Reef resorts. From Cairns there is scheduled service to Green Island several times a day and excursion service to Fitzroy Island along with Green, but these are mainly day trips. From Townsville, there are regular ferries to Magnetic Island. Heron Island has launch service from Gladstone. In the Whitsunday Group, there are ferries from Shute Harbor to many of the area resorts (although getting to Shute Harbor will require bus or taxi service from Proserpine or Whitsunday Field). Otherwise boat connectio ns are intermittent and poor, schedules change, and prices are so high that, not withstanding the cost, the time savings of flying almost always are most persuasive.

This is not to say that you will not find many references to launch and ferry connections in Australian Tourist Commission publications. What we mean is that you should keep a map handy when referring to travel promotion literature about Queensland. You may read, for example, that there is launch service to Dunk Island from Clump Point. The problem is that Clump Point is not really a place. It is a jetty several miles from any town and reachable by once or twice a day bus service along the coast or by taxi from the town of Mission Beach, which itself is not regularly served by any scheduled air service, and is about midway between Cairns and Townsville. Similarly, there is regular ferry service between Great Keppel Island and Rosslyn Bay, which is many miles and a difficult journey from the nearest scheduled air service at Rockhampton – fine for locals, but difficult for visiting Americans.

Within single groups of nearby islands, it is sometimes possible to arrange boat connections. Since fuel costs for ocean boating are not inconsequential, however, charter fees may prove high. Moreover, such connections are sometimes very weather sensitive, for you are now leaving the sheltered bays of island resorts and crossing open waters where tides and winds may influence whether a particular type of boat can make the journey comfortably.

It takes just under an hour for a launch to travel between Dunk Island and Hinchinbrook Island. It took the staff at the reception desk longer than that to think of a way of getting between the two resorts without going back to the coast and renting a car. There is no organized service connecting these resorts, so you must hire a water taxi for the trip if you wish to go directly. One water taxi company out of Mission Beach serving Dunk Island didn't want to make this trip.The other two taxis gave us quotes, and the low tariff for our trip was a rather stiff $A160. The advantage was that the connection cut out a wasted day of travel and incidentally offered a beautiful trip past several islands along the way. The price for two was not that unreasonable, considering that there would also have been water taxi and ground transportation costs to make the same connection by returning to the coast.

THE GREAT BARRIER REEF

Similar boat trips are feasible between Hinchinbrook and Orpheus Islands or between Brampton Island and any number of Whitsunday Group resorts. While many resorts commonly offer day charters which visit other islands, the boat transportation services connecting resort islands are quite rare and require special arrangements.

There is regular bus service along the Queensland coast. This is generally more advisable for coastal sightseeing, rather than island hopping. Locals scoffed at the idea of relying upon rail connections, although they ostensibly do exist. There are car rental agencies (multi-nationals such as Hertz, Avis and Budget, as well as local companies) in all of the major cities and towns of Queensland, but be sure to book ahead during the busy holiday seasons. *Your U.S. or Canadian driver's license is accepted for holiday driving in Australia.* Drop-off charges are not as bad as in the United States. The Bruce Highway along the Queensland coast is a well paved and graded two-lane road. Don't expect U.S. style freeways, however. It is by no means straight, and curves about as much as the coastline. You should also anticipate considerable slow agricultural traffic. Driving time is accordingly somewhat longer than you might expect for comparable U.S. trips.

In planning your journey to and between islands, keep the distances in mind. Although not unreasonable by American standards, they are longer than you might expect since Australia is a very large country. For most Americans wishing to plan an easy vacation, it will probably prove simplest to select a resort or combination of resorts with reasonable air access. If you wish to enjoy the adventure of some very scenic launch or light plane trips, however, arranging your own way as you go (since advance bookings will be virtually impossible) is fairly easy, although a tad expensive. You will find the Queenslanders anxious to facilitate your journey as best they can.

ATTIRE

Life at all Great Barrier Reef resorts is very informal. This means different things at different islands, however. At Orpheus Island, for example, they do ask that bathing suits be the minimum attire ,unless you seek out one of their more secluded beaches. On the other hand, at this elegant resort many people choose to dress rather nicely for dinner.

Expect to wear shorts or a bathing suit all day and light tropical clothes in the evening. Tee shirts or beach covers are vital in the daytime for sun protection and the occasional rain shower. Buy a souvenir hat or sun visor there. Bring a pair of comfortable sandals or thongs. Sand and paved walkways get very hot in the direct tropical sun, and, especially if your feet are sensitive, it can be miserable walking from room to beach or boat across the desert sand.

Some resorts have dress-up nights. A few others are unconcerned if you wear your bathing suit to the dinner table. Guests at most seem to have set a relaxed standard of unpretentious informal dress for dinner. Although we have tried to give you a feeling for each of the resorts, if you plan to visit more than one you should plan to bring suitable light casual evening wear.The temperature is most commonly such (except very occasionally during the winter – June and August – when there may be tropical breezes or very occasional stormy winds) that you rarely will want to wear long sleeves even in the evening, unless you are at one of the few air conditioned resort dining rooms, or want to dress up a bit.

For men, any shirt with collar (and we definitely recommend short sleeves for most evenings because of the temperature and humidity) will generally do. Short sleeve dress shirts and pull-over golf-type shirts are equally acceptable, worn with cotton or linen slacks or walking shorts. In the case of shorts, all resorts requested that gentlemen wear long socks. We saw some blue jeans, but lighter weights and lighter colors were worn by the overwhelming majority. Jackets are not required, and were only rarely seen.

For women, light blouses or tops with a wrap around or similar casual skirt or slacks and open shoes are appropriate. Cottons and synthetics greatly outnumbered silks, presumably because of the presence of laundries and the absence of dry cleaning facilities on virtually all of the islands. Stockings were a matter of personal preference.

Don't overpack. Perhaps because tipping is rare in Australia (airport porters are paid a flat rate per piece carried), there aren't a lot of porters around. You may find you have to hustle your own bags between airlines, and perhaps a bit more than when travelling in the U.S. or Europe. We have now taken to carrying a heavy duty collapsible suitcase trolley with us wherever we travel, and we were particularly happy we had it in Australia. The less you pack, the less you carry – and the more room you have in your suitcase for souvenirs.

Every resort sells tee shirts for anywhere from $A8 to $A16, depending on quality and fabric. They make fine souvenirs or gifts. There are some very nice and quite unusual pure cotton shirts made in China, and others from Singapore in styles we had not seen any where else. There are also tee shirt dresses, over long pullovers, which women can wear either belted or unbelted as poolside coverups or for informal evening wear, ranging in price from $A10 to $A30, again depending on style and fabric. If you wish, you can acquire much of what you might need for daytime wear as you go along.

Since you live in bathing suits and sandals at most resorts, neither men nor women need as much in the way of underwear and socks or stockings as for other vacations. Australians commonly wear shorts with long socks and shoes as town business attire during the day. Such dress is perfectly appropriate and far more comfortable than long trousers in the heat for travel throughout Queensland – on air planes, boats, in cities and towns, and certainly at any resort where you will delete the socks and shoes during the day. The availability of free or coin laundries at most of the resorts means you don't even have to rely on handwashing if you plan to be away for any length of time. Most resorts provide irons either in the room (Hamilton) or with the laundry facilities, so you can even look well pressed if you wish.

In winter (June-August) one sweater or lightweight jacket may be comfortable and useful in the event of occasional cooler, balmy evening breezes.

You will never have occasion to need fancy dress shoes. Men should have a comfortable and versatile pair of shoes for walking and evening wear – perhaps topsiders or some other similar boating or sport shoes – and a pair of tennis or jogging shoes which can double for walking, reef exploring and casual wear. Inexpensive resort shoes in whites or beige are more than adequate for evenings at any resort, and they have the added virtue of being lighter and easier to pack. Women may want a second pair of sandals to be worn in the evening, tennis or jogging shoes, and a good walking shoe. Dressy high heels are rarely seen.

Resort stores generally all and at least a basic selection of toiletries, and all offered at least a limited selection of vacation wear for those who arrived without suitable clothing. Sun lotions are abundantly available, albeit slightly expensive, and insect repellent is plentiful. On the other hand, such items as contact lens solutions, varied brands of cosmetics, or even antihistamines (for the cold we brought with us on the airplane) and other over-the-counter remedies were scarce, although they were much more readily available at *chemist* shops in coastal towns such as Cairns and Townsville. Unless you are planning to travel extensively along the coast, however, you had better plan to bring important personal times along with you.

on Great Keppel Island

Photographic opportunities abound, so bring your favorite camera. Remember that tropical daylight is intensely light, so beware of *back- lighting* (when the scene you're shooting has a lot of light behind it, when your foreground is dark and the background is light). These situations invariably trick your automatic lightmeter and give you pictures with murky dark subject matter and a bright burst of background light. Remember to set the light meter on the main subject of your picture, and *not* on the sun reflecting off water or the intensely bright sky.

As with any vacation resort, familiar brands of film are readily available and expensive. There are even one-day processing stores in most coastal towns and all major cities. If you bring film, most professionals recommend that you carry it in readily available lead lined film bags to protect it against airport x-ray examination. Examination is used sporadically in Australia for passengers boarding jet flights.

If you intend to dive or snorkel, try to bring some sort of underwater camera. Your choices begin with a relatively inexpensive camera – either an instamatic model (Minolta or Hanimex instamatic type in the under $125 range), or the Hanimex 35 mm. (around $200). As an alternative you may elect a simple underwater housing [Ewa, price around $50, to more sophisticated equipment in the $200 range] for an instamatic or other camera which allows you to take your regular camera to sea. For the serious photographer, the Nikonos V (camera and lens around $500), will cost closer to $1000, or perhaps more, when the ensemble is completed with proper flash equipment. Remember that virtually all underwater photography is flash photography because water of any depth quickly begins to filter color and intensity out of sunlight.

For battery operated flash units, you may be using quite a bit of electricity, so you may want to bring one or more spare sets of batteries along, depending on how fast you go through film.

South Molle Island

What do you need to do to get ready, aside from packing your clothes, to have a perfect trip? Don't forget your *passport*. Americans also must obtain an *Australian visa* from their embassy in Washington, or one of their consular offices. If you appear in person with a photograph, the process generally takes one day. If you have them send you an application and mail it to them with a return envelope, expect it to take two weeks or longer. The visas are good for trips up to six months in length and are valid for two years.

If you haven't prepared for the sun adequately, or if you otherwise require medical assistance, you will have to pay for your health care since Australian national health insurance does *not* cover foreign visitors. Currently, of all the Great Barrier Reef resorts, only Outrigger Resort on Hamilton Island has a resident physician. The others have dispensaries or nursing care available and arrange for health care with mainland physicians. As far as prescription medication, you can legally bring up to four weeks supply of prescription medicine into Australia without a doctor's certificate authorizing a larger amount. An endorsement by an Australian doctor for a prescription issued in North America will enable an Australian pharmacist to fill a prescription in Australia.

That's it! You are travelling to a place much like home, and there's virtually nothing you might be planning to carry along that you can't lay your hands on somehow in Cairns, Townsville, and especially Sydney or Melbourne.

white-capped noddies nest in the Pisonia trees

THINGS TO KNOW

WEATHER

When you cross the equator, the seasons are reversed. Therefore, while we shiver in December, Australians enjoy their summer, and it's a peculiar experience to see Santa Claus in short sleeves and lightweight clothes. On the other hand, Australia's ski season is at its peak in July or August. The Great Barrier Reef region is firmly in tropical climes, however. Winds in tropical latitudes tend to travel to where the sun is directly overhead, and during the Barrier Reef's winter the sun is far to the north over the Tropic of Cancer. From later April through to September or October, the Reef's climate is in its most benign mood, and this is when many Australians escape their own winter and migrate to the North Queensland coast.

In summer (January to March) the sun is over the Tropic of Capricorn, actually south of much of the Barrier Reef area, creating distinctly tropical weather patterns for the islands. Sudden heavy rain storms are possible, and thunderstorms can stir up brief, wild winds. Nonetheless, the weather is generally hot and pleasant, and many Queensland (in addition to a substantial population of southerners) plan their Christmas and New Year's holidays at the Reef's resorts.

Apart from the statistically remote possibility of a hurricane (every few years, usually with several day's warning) and few humid summer months, the Reef weather is usually beautiful. Periods of high humidity are common in the summer wet season (again, remember this means February), but rain is by no means a constant phenomenon during this period. Often it may rain for a part of a day and then clear. Occasionally in February or

THE GREAT BARRIER REEF

March it storms for as long as a few days and then clears. In any event, it tends to remain quite warm, and the rain is frequently a welcome respite from the temperatures of the tropical summer. As with most resorts in the tropics, the optimum time to travel for best weather conditions in the opinion of many experienced travelers is usually spring or fall – which in Australia would be around October–November and April-May, when weather conditions in the islands are generally sunny and brushed by languid light winds.

Resort Weather on the Great Barrier Reef
(monthly highs, lows, average rainfall)

	Jan	Feb	Mar	Apr	May	Jun	July	Aug	Sep	Oct	Nov	Dec
highs	89	88	87	84	81	78	77	80	82	85	87	88
lows	74	75	72	71	68	65	62	64	66	69	72	74
rainfall	15.7	17.4	18.3	7.0	3.6	2.0	1.2	1.0	1.4	1.4	3.3	6.7

Average total sunshine hours per month:
July-January 220
February -June 190

Average daily mean humidity: 75-80%

Australia uses the metric system for weights, measures and temperature. They used to use feet and inches, so Australians often express distances in miles as well as kilometers, yards as well as meters, and will understand you when you do too. So you will know, however, you can quickly *approximate* American measurements if you multiply kilometers by .6 to calculate miles, centimeters by 2.5 to get inches, and meters by .9 to get yards. Kilograms are 2.2 pounds. You very occasionally may see a few weights expressed in the English measurement of *stone* .These are 14 pounds, and we do not know any easy way to multiply by 14.

Australians refer to liters, rather than quarts and gallons, but so long as you remember that a liter is roughly a quart – 1.057 quarts to be more precise, but close enough for buying wine – you can get by just fine. Gasoline is generally sold by the liter, so don't applaud the amazingly low prices until you multiply them by 3.8 to convert to gallon prices.Australians are least familiar with the Fahrenheit temperature scale, so you should be prepared to speak Centigrade with them. When you hear the high temperature forecast for the day is 30º, you should be shedding most of your clothes. It's going to hit 86º Fahrenheit.

Centigrade	Fahrenheit
20	68
25	77
30	86
35	95
40	104

To calculate Fahrenheit from centigrade, divide the centigrade reading by 5, multiply by 9, and add 32 to the total. Every 10º centigrade is 18º Fahrenheit.

Incidentally, don't expect long range weather forecasts for northern Queensland. Australia depends heavily on U.S. satellite for weather information, and by the time it reaches Australia and gets interpreted for the southern hemisphere, it isn't sufficiently long-range any more. Particularly for limited population areas like the Barrier Reed region, there isn't the type of several days' advance prediction we have in the United States. This inability to predict tomorrow's high temperatures obviously won't affect your vacation particu- larly, but it does create a more uncertain situation for yachters who want to plan ahead, but cannot always tell from whence the next day's wind will blow.

Hamilton Island

From the Pacific Coast between *November* and *April,* Queensland is +18 hours relative to Pacific standard time. The easiest way to convert is to subtract 6 hours from West Coast time and add a full day. From *May* through *October,* when the United States is on daylight savings time, the Great Barrier Reef is +17 hours, or convert by subtracting 5 and adding a full day. The reason for this seeming anomaly – that when we set our clocks *ahead* for daylight time we actually reduce that time is determined relative to Universal Mean Time in Greenwich, England. We are *behind* UMT and come an hour closer when we go on daylight savings, while Australia is a *ahead* of UMT, so our daylight time catches us up an hour on the Australians.

To confuse matters further, much of Australia including Sydney, Melbourne, and most major cities outside Queensland – observes daylight saving time during *their* summer months. Sydney is then +19 – subtract 5 and add a day – when they are on daylight savings time and we are off (November to March), +18 – subtract 6 and add a day – when both Australia and the U.S. are on daylight savings time, and add 17 – and subtract 7 and add a day – when we are on daylight savings time and they are off (May through October).

These calculations are all given from the West Coast. For other time zones in the United States, *diminish,* the hourly difference accordingly (remember, you are closer to Greenwich, England, as you move eastward across the U.S.); when the Barrier Reef is +18 hours ahead of San Francisco, it is +17 to Denver, +16 to Chicago and +15 to New York. If this is all too much bother, consult the chart, lie on the beach and leave your watch at home.

GREAT BARRIER REEF

on Great Keppel Island

U.S. and Barrier Reef Time Differences

(U.S. *not* on daylight savings time)

San Francisco	Denver	Chicago	New York	Barrier Reef
[Monday]	[Monday]	[Monday]	[Monday]	[Tuesday]
6:00am	7:00am	8:00am	9:00am	midnight
8:00am	9:00am	10:00am	11:00am	2:00am
10:00am	11:00am	noon	1:00pm	4:00am
noon	1:00pm	2:00pm	3:00pm	6:00am
2:00pm	3:00pm	4:00pm	5:00pm	8:00am
4:00pm	5:00pm	6:00pm	7:00pm	10:00am
6:00pm	7:00pm	8:00pm	9:00pm	noon
8:00pm	9:00pm	10:00pm	11:00pm	2:00pm
10:00pm	11:00pm	*midnight	*1:00am	*4:00pm
*midnight	*1:00am	*2:00am	*3:00am	*6:00pm

(U.S. *on* daylight time)

San Francisco	Denver	Chicago	New York	Barrier Reef
[Monday]	[Monday]	[Monday]	[Monday]	[Tuesday]
6:00am	7:00am	8:00am	9:00am	*11:00pm
8:00am	9:00am	10:00am	11:00am	1:00am
10:00am	11:00am	noon	1:00pm	3:00am
noon	1:00pm	2:00pm	3:00pm	5:00am
2:00pm	3:00pm	4:00pm	5:00pm	7:00am
4:00pm	5:00pm	6:00pm	7:00pm	9:00am
6:00pm	7:00pm	8:00pm	9:00pm	11:00am
8:00pm	9:00pm	10:00pm	11:00pm	1:00pm
10:00pm	11:00pm	*midnight	*1:00am	3:00pm
*midnight	*1:00am	*2:00am	*3:00am	5:00pm

* indicates same day in U.S. and the Barrier Reef

GREAT BARRIER REEF

Telephone connections between the United States and Australia are excellent. Considering how long it often takes mail to reach the far north coast of Australia, investing $10 or so in phone calls can be well worth it, especially considering the very friendly reception Americans almost invariably get when they call the Great Barrier Reef area.

For U.S. cities having international direct dialing service (IDDS), Australia is easily and quickly reached by dialing 011 61. (The *international access code* is 011, and Australia's *country code* is 61.) Then dial the Australian area code – numbers in North Queensland are generally area code 70 to 79. (Note that in Australia you may see the area code written as **070** because in other parts of the country they have one-, two- and three-number area codes, but in dialing from the US, that initial **0** in their area code is omitted. Lastly, dial the five to seven digit (in northern Queensland, usually six digit) local number. For example, to call the Queensland Government Tourist Bureau in Cairns simply dial 011 61 70 51 3588#. (The U.S. telephone company recommends that # at the end of the number on touch-tone phones to speed the call through.)

It is generally quite easy to call from Australia to the United States. From the larger cities, most hotel rooms have telephones permitting direct dialing with charges added to your hotel bill. We saw no indication in Queensland of heavy surcharges of the type exacted by European and other international hotels, but you should ask the hotel operator before calling what the particular hotel's policy is. We did encounter substantial difficulties, however, having calls billed to our United States telephone credit cards, although we were continually assured that it could be done if we would just wait until arrangements were made. It was much faster and easier just to make the calls and pay for them there.

Australian pay phones, incidentally, are somewhat different than ours, but are pretty clearly explained on the instructions at each station, so no need to feel intimidated. Just make sure you have a handful of 20 cent coins, and you will have little difficulty. You will have to get used to a different set of dial and busy signals, but that's easy. One nice thing on the newer phones – you deposit your coins and, after your party answers, meters on the phone calculate the charges during your call and display how much money you have left on your toll call.

on Lizard Island

on Bedarra Island

on Dunk Island

LIFESTYLE

FOOD and DRINK

The Great Barrier Reef area offers some excellent culinary and gustatory opportunities. All food is very edible. Health standards are enforced at a very high level. Quality beef, lamb, shellfish and seafood are available, and most resorts and local restaurants serve the finest ingredients.

Resort breakfast generally is English style with selections of meats, toasts, pancakes, fish, bacon, sausages and the like in addition to fruits, juices and cereals. Lunches are served at the table at a few of the smaller resorts, but more generally are buffet style. Dinners are generally four course, or larger affairs: soup, entrée (which in Australia is an introductory course), main course and dessert.

You will find a fine selection of fresh tropical fruits to begin the day, and with most meals. North Queensland is rich in mango particularly. There is also abundant banana, pineapple, paw paw (papaya), kiwi and passion fruit. While coconut appears to grow abundantly, it is not commonly served or used in Australian cuisine.

There are several things, in particular different types of seafood, which are somewhat new to most Americans but which are an absolute must on a Barrier Reef trip. *Bugs* (also called Bay Lobster) from Moreton Bay near Brisbane in South Queensland are an odd-shaped, but exquisite, scampi-sized lobster (rarely over 6" in total length including their strange flat head), eaten just like their larger cousins by removing the shell and feasting on the tail. This delicacy was discovered in the 1950s when new methods of trawling for prawns were devised.

Only later was it recognized that these were not the unpleasant tasting Balmain bugs, but were a delicious new find. Until then these small creatures were in such abundance they were considered a nuisance, and were often thrown away rather than consumed. The Moreton Bay bugs are particularly memorable when grilled simply and served with a garlic butter sauce.

If you have ever enjoyed the hard shell Dungeness crab of which San Franciscans are so proud, you'll love the Queensland *mud crabs,* one of Australia's biggest crustaceans, occasionally growing to four pounds. Don't be put off by the *mud* in their name. They are generally found in the mangrove tree swamps, and are also called *mangrove crab.* These delicious creatures are about the same size as the Pacific Coast variety, have large bodies and major claws but lack the smaller meaty legs of the American variety. Although Australians serve these crabs either hot or cold, they are particularly superb cold with either mayonnaise or melted butter, accompanied by a new Australian chablis or Chardonnay or, if you prefer beer, one of the light Queensland lagers.

Queensland is fresh prawn country. *Prawn* trawlers can be seen working the channels and bays up and down the coast, and many of them sell part of their catch to nearby resort kitchens before snap-freezing the rest right aboard the fishing boat. The frozen catch is processed and then shipped all over the world. Australians most often serve their fresh prawns whole – whether hot or cold, so don't be surprised to see head and tails, and expect to do a bit of work in the eating process. The trawlers also often bring in abundant catches of small *squid*, so the restaurants frequently offer fried or sautéed calamari.

The Australian *rock lobster tail* which has become almost a cliché item on American restaurant menus, comes from the south, quite a distance from the Barrier Reef, and may not be available fresh in the north. Some friends of ours had trouble finding it fresh in Sydney and were told it was virtually all being exported to the U.S. From closer to the north coast, however, there are very similar *crayfish* which are almost indistinguishable from the southern variety. Either makes a superb lobster dinner.

The *barramundi* is probably one of the best cooking fish in the world. It is a moderately large fish, caught in northern Australian rivers, with thick succulent fillets. A close runner-up is the *coral trout,* which you may catch in the waters off many Barrier Reef islands. There are also excellent *coral salmon* and *bass*. Slightly more abundant is the *sweetlip,* which in some areas are so common they will almost take a hook without bait. Large *mackerel* are also common, especially in the Whitsunday Passage. Even the dishes served as *reef fish*, or whatever the fishing crew caught this morning, are a complete pleasure.

Beef is a major product of Queensland which boasts some of the largest cattle *stations* in the world. Interestingly we found less chicken or other poultry then one would expect, and the lamb, although locally produced, is more commonly served on the breakfast hot table, and we felt it was almost invariably poorly prepared. We were impressed by the quality of the locally grown vegetables from the tablelands west and south or Cairns. Desserts are of the familiar variety and generally quite enjoyable, although we didn't particularly care for the *Pavlova,* which we were told is the *national dessert*. It is a mixture of meringue and whipped cream, very rich, but monotonous.

THE GREAT BARRIER REEF

Australian beers are known world-wide. The local brew in the far north is *Cairns' NQ* (North Queensland) Lager, although as you proceed south among the islands more people seem to prefer the *4-X* from Brisbane or the beer which is most familiar to Americans, *Fosters*.

Many Americans are unaware that Australia is a major wine producing nation, with many quality products well worth becoming acquainted with. They do tend to drink their wines quite young, so don't be surprised if you're offered a wine bearing a label with the same vintage as the date on your plane ticket. Their principle wine growing regions are to the south: Hunter Valley (around 130 miles north of Sydney), Griffith area (400 miles from Sydney), Barossa Valley (starting 30 miles northeast of Adlelaide) and Swan Valley (north-east of Perth). Less well known are Rutherglen and the Goulburn Valley (near Melbourne) and the Clare and Watervale districts (20 miles north of Adelaide).

Australian varietals include some familiar and some less well known, in the United States. Among whites, their chablis is much closer to the French product, with less body but possessing a hearty Chardonnay character. Australian chardonnays, on the other hand, have much of the bold fruitiness associated with California chardonnays, generally without the earthy character of the traditional French white burgundies.

The most common Australian *house white* is called a Riesling, although in fact it is commonly produced chiefly from semillon grapes. Australia is starting to produce a true Riesling, but these are not yet widely offered. Some bars also offer a domestic Mosel by the glass or carafe, but this is generally far too sweet for most people's taste. The bulk Riesling, though, is generally very acceptable – indeed much more so than many wines served routinely in bars and restaurants in the U.S. – and is quite modest in price.

As for reds, Australian wines need a bit more development in our opinion. A good Aussie shiraz (also labeled Hermitage) can be a pleasant find, and we enjoyed a couple of their young light pinot noirs. The cabernet sauvignon in our estimation, however, needs more development before they will share the limelight with their California or Bordeaux cousins.

In addition to the general selection of drinks in your room refrigerator, the dining rooms and bars will be pleased to sell you drink supplies to take to your room. At many resorts you can, if you wish, buy a box of Riesling to put in the refrigerator. Yes, we said *box* , for it is Australia which appears to have dominated the industry which markets bulk wine in cardboard boxes with reinforced foil liners. At $A10 for four liters – remember, that's about a gallon – the wine is really quite inexpensive, yet surprisingly drinkable.

All of the resorts are *fully licensed* (unlike some restaurants in towns and even large cities, where you must bring your own drinks) and generally have full bar and wine and beer selections. Drinks are very fairly priced by U.S. standards ($A0.80 - $A1.25 for a glass of wine at the bar), and the bartenders will keep a running tab for guests during their stay.

TIPPING

Almost all Australians, perhaps excepting people in service industries, like the fact that theirs is not a tipping society. They hope visiting Americans won't ruin it for them. No service charges are added to restaurant or hotel bills.

The typical Australian does not tip for normal meal service. If he or she wants to recognize special service, it is generally accepted that 10% of the bill is sufficient. Australians hardly ever tip a taxi driver unless special help is rendered with luggage or some other difficulty. Hotel bellmen are salaried and will deliver bags to your room without sticking their hands out for gratuities. Say *thank you* and they will depart. Airport porters charge per piece carried and do not expect a tip from Australians.

Everyone, however, has learned that Americans do tip, so a fraction of your drivers, porters and waiters may linger to give you the chance to follow *your* custom rather than theirs. Don't be intimidated. Tip if you wish, but don't feel it is required.

AMENITIES

Less than a third of the Great Barrier Reef resorts have television sets, radios or even an alarm clock in their rooms. Then again, who needs alarm clocks when one of nature's best alarms, an incredible array of tropical birds, announces the dawn for all who want to be up and about during the coolest part of the day. If you are interested in having a radio, consider bringing a small shirt pocket size AM battery operated radio.

Listening to Queensland's AM radio stations out of Carins, Townsville, Mackay or Brisbane is both fun and informative.

If you want to listen to Radio Australia and other national shortwave broadcasts to and from the southeastern part of the world, consider buying one of the newer battery operated radios which effectively pick up AM, FM and short wave, yet weigh only a matter of ounces. Prices for these technological wonders in the U.S. range from $75 to $250 depending on refinements, including such things as automatic shut-off and digital clocks which make the small wonder into a fine clock radio you may be able to make use of at home.

Few resorts have telephones in the rooms. Daydream Island does, but goes through a central switchboard. Hayman, South Molle and Hamilton Islands have dial telephones in the rooms. All four of these resort are in the Whitsunday Group. Dunk and South Molle have two pay phones at each resort. At both, the reception offices close at 5:00, so incoming phones calls must be arranged during business hours. Deux Orpheus Island had but one phone on the entire island. Located in the office, it is shared by receptionist, management and guests.

At the island resorts without room phones, if you are expecting incoming calls, advise the staff. In most instances they will be very cooperative in allowing you to receive brief calls in the office. For the most part, however, these are distinctly not resorts where you can keep in close touch with the office, and are for those who want to leave such things behind. But then, that's why you're travelling 7500 miles or more, isn't it?

At most resorts, you are given a room key at check in time (a few resorts don't even bother), but you will never use it at most, so you might as well leave it in the room at all but the very largest hotels. Only in one particularly large resort did we even hear of even a hint of a problem, and that involved staff and resort property rather than any guest possessions. Australians do not appear particularly security conscious, and we saw no reason for them to be so in most vacation areas.

Electricity throughout Australia is 240/250 volts. Australia uses a unique three-pronged plug for its appliances.The bottom vertical prong is the ground, and the top two are the *hot* plugs. If your appliances are grounded and do not pose a shock risk, you can get by using just the top two prongs.

These top two are what make Australia so different. They look like they started with an American plug then twisted the bottom of each prong to the outside about 30. Best not to try twisting your appliance plugs to fit their sockets, particularly since most American appliances now have one prong larger than the other because we build in our grounds differently. Your appliance plug may not fit their socket, and you will have a messed up situation when you return home.

Electronic supply stores, and appliance stores catering to international clientele, carry adaptors which will let you plug in your hair dryer, radio or whatever in Australia. If you have bought an international converter set, it probably came with one of these widgets. Call your nearest Australian consulate or national tourist office if you cannot track one down. Do, however, try to bring at least one with you, since hotels and resorts never seem to have any available.

Otherwise, Australian and particularly Barrier Reef amenities are much like home. Everything is very clean by our standards.

Bathrooms ranging from plain to outstanding are as you would expect them in comparable northern hemisphere facilities from national parks to exotic resorts. *Outrigger Resort at Hamilton Island,* for example, provides wall- mounted electric hair dryers in every bathroom – something we had not seen in the U.S. or Europe. Most resorts provide electric irons, either in the room or in conjunction with laundry facilities, so you may not need that travel iron. One thing *every* Australian resort offers – it must be a law – is an electric pot for heating water for instant coffee or tea in your room, and an ample supply of both.

MONEY and CREDIT

The Australian dollar ($A), like the U.S. counterpart, is 100 cents. There are coins worth 1, 2, 5, 10, 20 and 50 cents (the last a fascinating 12-sided coin identical in size and shape to the Fijian 50 cent), as well as a gold-colored $1 coin. Australian currency comes in 2, 5, 10, 20, 50 and 100 dollar bills of differing colors. You can, if you wish, acquire Australian currency and Australian dollar travelers' checks in the United States from Thomas Cook offices or most any urban currency exchange. Sydney's Kingsford Smith airport has a large banking facility just as you exit customs. Cairns' airport, however, has much more limited facilities, and the bank could be closed when you arrive.

Every resort accepted more than one of the familiar major credit cards. Lizard Island wants American Express or Diners, but Visa and Mastercard were accepted everywhere else as well (except, for some mysterious reason, the resort store on Daydream Island was not equipped for Mastercard).

73

THE GREAT BARRIER REEF

As a practical matter, there is little need to carry cash or credit cards with you while on the resort premises. Everything in the way of food, drink, supplies, souvenirs and excursions can be charged to your room bill. An exception is Great Keppel Island, where many of the activities are independent of the resort, and for reasons which entirely escaped us, management would not collect for the day-charters, but advised guests to carry cash with them.

on Dunk Island

In giving resort and other prices we have relied heavily on their published prices. While we were at resorts we discussed prices with management and tried to get them to project their prices as far into the future as possible. Obviously, though, when you plan your trip it is possible things may have changed. To avoid any confusion over exchange rates, all figures given as $A are in Australian dollars and, unless indicated to the contrary, are *per person* for twin/double occupancy. Resorts in the Barrier Reef area generally impose a hefty surcharge – 50% or more – for single occupancy. There is no universally agreed high or low *season* in the Barrier Reef. Most resorts increase prices during heavy holiday periods like Christmas-New Year season, and others have higher rates at other times of the year.

The other side of the coin, however, is that most resorts offer ways to save a few dollars. Almost all, and particularly those in which TAA or Ansett have an ownership interest ,offer package rates combining air fare from Melbourne, Sidney or Brisbane. At the time of this writing, they had not yet started offering packages via Cairns or Townsville, but we expect they will shortly. If your plans are such that you will be visiting only one or two islands in the region, and you will be travelling from one of the principal cities, be sure to check with your travel agent, airline or resort directly for information regarding reduced package rates.

Several resorts offer *standby* rates. These apply if you call within 48 hours of your planned arrival and inquire about available space. It is a clever device of the resorts for filling otherwise empty rooms and will save you at least 15%, and often considerably more, from the cost of accommodations and meals. This is a devise used by many resorts, particularly in the Whitsunday Group.

Hayman Island

ISLANDS OF THE GREAT BARRIER REEF

In this chapter, we discuss each of the island resorts of the Great Barrier Reef, and a few incidentally interesting islands without resorts. In deciding on the order in which to list them, we had several choices (favorites, north-to-south, price, and so forth) and took the easy way out. They are *listed alphabetically* for convenient reference, since we have no way knowing whether you are looking for a single island on which to vacation, a group of islands, the whole string, or even which gateway through which you might be entering.

Since the Australians did not name the islands alphabetically in geographical order, we have prepared the following list to give you several pieces of information in condensed form. The resort islands are listed running from north to south. With each, we have indicated the approximate size of the island, number of accommodations, and price range of accommodation offered at their resort. Except as indicated to the contrary, note that prices are for *full board* (three meals) for *two people* per day.

Unfortunately, prices change over time. We have done our best to get the most current information at press time. We of course cannot anticipate how developments on a couple of islands planning major changes will affect rates.

Hamilton Island

THE GREAT BARRIER REEF

island/resort	size	accommodations	price range
Lizard	(3.9 sq. miles)	30 rooms	$A300-420
Green	(3.2 acres)	29 units	$A100-150
Fitzroy	(510 acres)	5units	$A150
Dunk	(4.7 sq. miles)	140 rooms	$A196-276
Bedarra	(250 acres)	14 bungalows	$A340
Hinchinbrook	(231 sq. miles)	30 cabins	$A170-190
Orpheus	(8.6 sq. miles)	25 rooms	$A280-320
Magnetic	(19 sq. miles)		

The Whitsunday Group

island/resort	size	accommodations	price range
Hayman	(1.5 sq. miles)	185 rooms	$A140-222
Daydream	(26 acres)	78 rooms	$A118-158
South Molle	(1.5 sq. miles)	202 rooms	$A160-180
Long	(257 acres)		
Whitsunday100		50 units	$A138
Palm Bay Resort		9 units	$A46.50 *without meals*
Hamilton	(2.4 sq. miles)	250 rooms today, but tomorrow?	A130-160 *without meals*
Lindeman	(3 sq. miles)	92 rooms	$A130-170

island/resort	size	accommodations	price range
Brampton	(195 acres)	100 rooms	$A108-160
Newry	(112 acres)		$A30 *without meals*
Great Keppel	(5.5 sq. miles)	140 rooms	$A150-158
Heron	(42 acres)	90 rooms	$A148-300
Lady Elliot	(112 acres)	43 units, packages only	
Fraser	(234 sq. miles)		

Bedarra

BEDARRA

- coral viewing • bushwalks • fishing
- tennis • golf • sailing • snorkeling
- swimming • horseback riding

THE GREAT BARRIER REEF

Officially designated Richards Island on navigation charts, Bedarra is located roughly equidistant from Cairns and Townsville. Bedarra, a corruption of an aboriginal word, is three miles from shore and the same distance south of Dunk Island. It is a relatively small island – just over a mile long – yet has eight very nice beaches and is even more beautiful from ashore than when viewed from the sea. It is one of the only islands in the Family Islands group which has abundant water coming from several natural springs. As a result, it can comfortably support its tiny resort facility.

Access to Bedarra Island is almost invariably by the *Big Red* launch from nearby Dunk Island (on an as-required basis) or occasionally directly by water taxi from South Mission Beach on the coast just opposite or by launch ($A12 round trip) from Clump Point. Air Queensland roundtrip fare from Cairns to Dunk is $A125.80.

Except for the northeastern corner which is still private property, this resort island is wholly owned by TransAustralia Airline, as is neighboring Dunk Island. *The emphasis here is on quiet relaxation.* You can expect to encounter more jungle fowl than people on the paths.

The Hideaway Resort ($A170 per person twin share per day includes all meals *and drinks*, with a large open bar and an open refrigerator chock full of beer, Australian wines, mineral waters and soft drinks in the dining area), is set just off the beach within a thick tropical forest with abundant orchids and other colorful flora. The resort currently has fourteen self-contained bungalows, some well spaced to insure privacy, and others two and three to a building. TAA has already announced plans, however, to move the entire resort to the other side of the island

and increase the size from fourteen to twenty-five to thirty bungalows. The exact location and shape the new resort will take is still in the design phase, but a TAA executive assured us the resort will still remain a *hideaway*.

At present, each medium sized unit has a double bed, little furniture (they do need a substantially larger dresser), a generous size bath room, ceiling fans, refrigerator, tea and coffee-making facilities, radio, and private intercom linking the guest rooms to the central complex (you'll probably have to ask for an explanation as to how it works, however). Rooms were done in pleasant light tile, but could use a bit more of the decorator's touch. There are laundry and ironing facilities available in the complex.

There is a large open bar and rustic dining area near the pool and the boat dock. A large hot breakfast is available. Lunch regrettably was always a meager buffet selection of cold cuts (rather routine salami, ham, pastrami, cheese with bread on request), one warm dish (quíche one day, curry another), and green salad with no dressing on the table. The evening meal here is rather like a casual dinner party. Guests are seated at very informal tables for six. This is fine if you wish to interact with other guests, but means there is no chance for an intimate dinner. Except for the pleasant buffet dinner with several roasts on the carving board, the other meals offered only a single main course with no choices. The kitchen and dining room were slightly understaffed. The very pleasant crew did yeoman work, but the service tended to be rather slow.

Guests at Bedarra have access to all of the island with the exception of the small portion of Bedarra which is not part of the resort and is still privately owned by a charming octogenarian artist who is entirely self-sustaining, and lives without electricity or regular outside supply.

There used to be some accommodations available in the old **Plantation** on the opposite end of the island, but it has fallen into disuse. These were old adobe style rooms with large patios amidst tropical flowers. Now there is only a young couple

Bedarra

acting as caretakers for the house, beautiful lawns and garden, and as hosts when **Dunk Island Resort** opens the **Plantation** to day guests, bringing a small boatload over five times a week to enjoy a barbecue luncheon.

This old house may well be the center point of the new resort, situated as it is between Hermandia Beach and Wedgerock Bay, both very attractive beaches. We hope the delightful old residence is kept in tact. The route for **Hideaway** guests to the **Plantation** is across the island and not along the shoreline; the beaches are not continuous, and it would be impossible to walk along the coast. One can boat around the island, of course. Be aware before undertaking the forty-five minute walk through rather dense forest, however, that the path is very poorly marked in places. We found that tying a handkerchief to a branch in one place was a reassuring way of guaranteeing that we would find our way back. It is a very pleasant jungle trek, passing the lookout just below the island's highest point, 350' *Allason Hill.*

Bedarra has some of its own recreation facilities, and shares others with its sister resort to which there are free launch transfers for registered guests. Catamaran sailing, snorkeling, small motor boats, swimming pool, paddle skis, cruises to the Outer Barrier Reef, hiking, and fishing are the principal activities on this quiet island. Nearby Timana Isle is the home of a well-known Australian artist who produces very distinctive woven tapestries and welcomes visitors from the resort.

One of the most pleasant and delightful things to do here is have the kitchen prepare a barbecue lunch for you. The staff will fill a cooler with steaks, sausages, chops – more than you can possibly eat – for you to take one one of the available dinghies.

THE GREAT BARRIER REEF

You can sail to one of the secluded beaches, gather some driftwood for a fire on the beach, and cook your lunch on a grill the staff will give you to take along. Don't forget some of that great Australian beer or wine from the refrigerator on your way to your boat.

No one will press activity on you at Bedarra. In fact, unlike other resorts, there is no activities board or list of things to do. Instead, you are pretty much on your own. The manager did invite all the guests for an afternoon catamaran sail around the island on an older boat which moors nearby. He neglected to mention, however, that there would be a $A15 per person charge for the ride added to your bill at check out.

Bedarra

All to the plus, however, for those seeking a *hideaway* such as this, there were no evening discos, no crowds, and a beautiful island. Indeed, our real criticism of the resort (other than things which obviously will be changed during the imminent renovation) is a rather laconic, *laid back* attitude on the part of management. For such an exclusive operation, they were rarely around during our stay. The small staff, however, positively bubbles with enthusiasm, and the hideaway idea is so pleasant and romantic that you overlook minor shortcomings. Bedarra can be the quietest escape among Barrier Reef resorts and, given its relative accessibility by air from Cairns via Dunk, may be just what you want for a brief get-away-from-it-all sojourn with next-door bustling activity available at nearby Dunk.

Bedarra Island is just beginning to gain recognition in its own right. Until now it has been a satellite of the Dunk Island resort, and has gotten much of its traffic from the small day excursions run from Dunk. When the new facility is designed and completed, TAA is sure to feature it even more. Reservations, already difficult to come by because of the resort's limited capacity, will undoubtedly become a matter of considerable advance planning or last-minute good luck. Fortunately, the resort is on the airline computer system, and you can check pretty easily for availability.

Hideaway Resort
via Dunk Island
via Townsville, Qld. 4810
[70] 688 168

Reservations through TransAustralia Airlines

luring fish to the surface

BRAMPTON

- coral viewing • national park
- bushwalks • fishing • waterskiing
- anchorage • tennis • golf • sailing
- snorkeling • windsurfing • swimming

CORAL SEA

Magnetic Is.
TOWNSVILLE
C. Cleveland
C. Bowling Green
C. Upstart
Bait Reef
Hook Reef
Hardy Reef
CUMBERLAND IS.
Eshelby Is.
Hayman Is.
Bowen
Port Denison
Hook Is.
Border Is.
Whitsunday Is.
Lupton Is.
Haslewood Is.
Shute Harbour
Pentecost Is.
Lindeman Is.
Whitsunday Passage
Long Is.
Sir J. Smith Group
The Great Barrier Reef
CAIRNS
Brampton Island
TOWNSVILLE
MACKA
MACKAY
ROCKHAMPTON
Prudhoe Is.
Northumberland Is.
QUEENSLAND
Middle Is.
BRISBANE
Percy Isles

THE GREAT BARRIER REEF

Situated just about 20 miles from Mackay, and reached by light aircraft or launch or air from Shute Harbor, this popular island is in the Cumberland Islands Group near Whitsunday Passage's southern entrance. Because of its distance from Lindeman, generally considered the southern-most resort among the Whitsunday Group resorts, Brampton does not get much traffic from charter boats in the Whitsunday Passage. Nor does it share much of the resort traffic through Shute Harbor or Hamilton Island.

In earlier days wild horses were bred on this island for use with the Indian army. It is a relatively large mountainous island with both open forest and rain-forest. The island boasts white sandy beaches and fringed coral. The top part of the island is a national park forest. Many have described this as the prettiest of the islands in the area.

Roylen Cruises, a family business, owned the island since 1962. In 1985 the family sold the entire resort to TransAustralia Airlines for 12 million. TAA's executives indicate that the new project will place an emphasis on *couples* , but beyond that there are no specifics available yet. For now TAA continues to operate the old facility. A launch operates from Mackay ($A12 one way) every day at 9:00 a.m. Air Queensland had daily 20 minute flights from Mackay ($37.00 one way) and Monday from Shute Harbor. A charming old train takes passengers from jetty to hotel.

Day visits to the island are possible. Cruises can also be arranged to other islands. Brampton is near Carlisle Island, separated by a narrow channel, with coral reefs viewable from glass-bottom boats at high tide, or wading at low tide.

Brampton Island Resort, with motel style units is a not-quite luxurious, informal resort. [$A54-80 per person includes meals.] It is known chiefly as *a place to relax on the beach.* All units are situated in shady settings in a coconut grove, originally

a secluded beach

planted in the last century to provide food for ship-wrecked mariners. Several types of accommodations serving a maximum of 218 guests are offered: **Bougan Villas** ($A43 per person per day, meals included ed), **Palm Villas** ($A54), **Carlisle Villas** ($A65), **Blue Lagoon units** ($A75), and **Suites** ($A80).The fancier holiday units are situated on shady pathways behind the beach. The resort has just added several new rooms and a new swimming pool.

Some fish nibble the coral polys, while others catch minute worms and other animals which live among the coral.

The dining room in the central complex is airconditioned, which is somewhat unusual among Barrier Reef resorts. Buffets and barbecues are featured frequently. There is a nightly party, a resident band at the cabaret, fancy dress nights, singalong and games nights.

Island activities include bushwalking, good fishing (the chef will cook what you catch), glass bottom boats, water skiing, aquaplane, swimming in the rock pool on the Eastern beach or the saltwater pool on North Beach, tennis and golf, and the usual resort activities. The resort has a game room, boutique and bank agency.

Brampton seems to charge for everything. An oyster bucket rented for fifty cents. Yet, they seem to have a clientele of people who come back year after year. Returning guests obviously come for the beautiful beaches and relaxed atmosphere, and by now they have learned to bring their own oyster buckets. What TAA will do with this island is still unknown. Since things have been getting a little frayed around the edges, however, it's possible that the change will do the old place lots of good.

Brampton Island
P.O. Box 169
Mackay, Qld. 4740
[79] 572 595

Reservations through McLeans Roylen Cruises, River Street Mackay, Qld. 4740; telephone [79] 572 595

Daydream Island

DAYDREAM

- coral viewing • national park
- bushwalks • fishing • waterskiing
- scuba diving • tennis • sailing
- snorkeling • windsurfing • swimming

THE GREAT BARRIER REEF

The brochure says it: *Daydream is a small tropical island– and the whole island is a resort – not just a resort on an island.* Part of the Whitsunday Island group, and known on the navigation charts as West Molle Island, Daydream was named after a cruising yacht well known in the area in the 1930's. It is indeed a very small lush tropical island – in fact, the smallest of the settled islands in the area –situated about two miles east of Shute Harbor within the Whitsunday Passage. Near the resort, the beaches are rocky, but at the north end of the island there is a superb white coral sand beach. Parts of the island are rainforest with very rich areas of beautiful vegetation.

Reached by launch from Shute Harbor (20 mins, $A10 round trip) which departs at 7:30 a.m., 9:00 a.m. and 5:00 p.m. daily, the resort will also arrange pick-up at Proserpine airport ($A25 transfer fee). On the way from Shute Harbor, you get a delightful tour of Whitsunday Passage, truly one of the most beautiful waterways in the world. Daydream provides very limited anchorage for visiting yachts on the back, or eastern side. There are day trips available to Daydream ($A20) which include barbecue lunch around the pool and all beach activities (water skiing $A3 extra).

Daydream was one of the first coral islands in this area to be developed for tourism. It is visited mainly by Australians and has not become very well known in the American market (so advises affable assistant manager Gail Witcher who has been in Australia 16 years, but still has a very detectable trace of Minnesota in her speech). Developed by Cobb & Co.(a Queensland-based bus company), the resort was purchased by Ansett Airlines when they bought Hayman, and was then demolished in 1952. Gold Coast entrepreneur Bernie Elsey purchased the lease from Ansett and developed the island for tourism in 1968. The resort was totally flattened by hurricane Ada in 1970, but was rebuilt with a fairly impressive and sturdy complex of motel-type units.

The hotel sits at the southern end of the island. It consists of two-story modern tropical wood frame buildings containing 78 units accommodating a maximum of 184 guests. Each room faces the beach to the front, and also has a view of Whitsunday passage from back windows.You certainly are aware that you're on an island here. There are three styles of accommodations, all with private bath, air-conditioning, refrigerators, tea and coffee maker, and most with television. Use of all island water facilities, except for water skiing and scuba diving, is included in the room rates without extra charge.

Poolside Suites ($A59 per person per day, all meals included) are downstairs around the large swimming pool. **Daydreamer Suites** ($A69) upstairs have even better views of the Whitsunday Passage. The six **VIP Suites** and the more elegant **Sunlover Lodge** (both $A79) are larger and have color television, full bath, rather than shower, and nicer amenities. Like several other Whitsunday area resorts, **Daydream** offers a stand-by rate ($A49) for people calling within 48 hours of their arrival and accepting accommodation on an as-available basis.

The resort has just undergone refurbishing and remodelling. It has a very comfortable and pleasantly appointed Polynesian decor restaurant and a cavernous bar lounge (with nightly live entertainment) for dancing, cabaret, fancy dress nights, *horse racing night* , talent quests, and other theme nights. There is a small downstairs *pub* where new guests are met by the management and oriented to the resort. Buffet breakfast, poolside barbecues for lunch, served dinners with a small, but adequate and very moderately priced, wine list. There is also a small coffee shop.

Activities include a large free-form swimming pool with a bar in the center, scuba instruction (including a free introductory lesson in the pool and intermediate training allowing you to dive with an instructor or dive master), badminton, cruises to other islands and the outer reef, fishing, a good all weather tennis court, volley ball, paddle skis, snorkeling, coral viewing from a private barge, six-person outrigger canoe, wind surfing, spa and sauna. You can walk or ride the motorboat to *Sunlovers Beach*, the beautiful small secluded beach area for sunbathing and snorkeling at the north end of the island. There are also beautiful walks through the tropical forest on the island. There is a small, well stocked store which will take virtually any credit card *except* Master Charge. There are coin laundry facilities.

As with most Whitsunday Group resorts, there are many opportunities to visit the other resorts in the immediate vicinity – particularly South Molle, and the proximity of Shute Harbor makes it fairly easy to traverse back and forth. This also allows you to take advantage of some of the day charters, such as reef excursions and fishing trips, based at nearby resorts.

Daydream Island Resort is what would have to be called a sleeper. Management is cordial, personable, and highly motivated to see that every guest has a good time. People are addressed by name whenever possible, and every effort is made to avoid the routine or institutional approach to resort life. It is a quiet resort and a relaxing island. If that's what you're in the mood for, this is one of those small, less expensive resorts that might well be the absolutely perfect base of operation for a great vacation.

Daydream Island Resort
Daydream Island
via proserpine. Qld. 4800
[79] 469 200

Reservations through Daydream Island, G.P.O. Box 918, Brisbane, Qld. 4001; telephone [7] 299 1961

Daydream Island

Humbug fish

DENT

• no resort • coral arts business

In the Whitsunday area, this long narrow island west of Hamilton Island has *no resort*. The manned lighthouse on the island was established in 1874. Septuagenarians Lene and Bill Wallace, retired Americans who have occupied the island for years, have established a *coral arts business* adjacent to the sandy beach just across from the Hamilton Island marina. Many people sail by and stop to see their work and relax on the island. The buildings are situated in a palm grove where one finds many strolling peacocks. The yacht anchorage, however, is poor, and the approach is easier on a small power boat.

on Dunk Island

DUNK

- coral viewing • national park• bushwalks
- fishing • waterskiing •anchorage • tennis
- golf • sailing • snorkeling • windsurfing
- swimming • horseback riding

THE GREAT BARRIER REEF

This large tropical island is located about 100 miles south of Cairns, about the same distance north of Townsville, and around two miles off the coast, opposite and within sight of the small town of Mission Beach. In the other direction, it is 15 miles from the Great Barrier Reef. Dunk, with its lush jungle and tropical rain forest, its fascinating giant butterflies, abundant beautiful tropical birds (including the exotic large white sulphur-crested cockatoo) and long palm-bordered sand beaches may well have the *best natural attributes* of all of the Barrier Reef resorts.

In 1896 journalist E.J. Banfield took a lease on the island and later was granted ownership of an agricultural homestead on which he and his wife lived until his death twenty years later, after gaining recognition as the author of several books on the joys of living as a beachcomber and lover of nature. The ownership of Dunk passed to others who later started to develop it seriously for tourism, building accommodations and ulti-mately carving an airstrip across the peninsula.

Dunk Island is one of Queeensland's more luxurious and sophisticated island resorts. It is the main island of the Family Group, having twelve islands in all, with Bedarra Island the other developed resort, still in its infancy, in the group.

Much of the island is rain forest, with dozens of varieties of tropical birds visible along the track leading to the summit of Mount Koo-ta-loo. Dunk beaches on the northern side of the island, feature unusually fine sand, which is quite uncommon on barrier reef islands. Much of Dunk island, particularly the rain forest, is protected national park.

The island is known for its magnificent, if somewhat elusive, giant butterflies, particularly the giant blue *Ulysses butterfly* (whose four to six inch wing spread has been exaggerated in fable, and tourism literature, to be twelve inches). Don't be disappointed if you only see smaller blue butterflies. Climb to the top of *Koo-ta-loo* along the fairly easy path (about two hours up and back), and you're almost certain to see a blue butterfly and yet one or another impressively large butterfly (quite possibly the lovely *Cairns Green Birdwing*) among the trees of the rain forest. If you do take this beautiful walk, remember that you are in the tropics where both temperature and humidity are higher than they feel. Because there are no facilities along the way, *take along some fruit or something to drink so you don't become dehydrated.*

Dunk is easily reached by air from Cairns by Air Queensland ($A62.90 each way for the forty-five minute trip) which operates several daily flights using DeHavilland Twin Otters. Air Queensland also has daily flights from Townsville using the same aircraft for about the same price. If you can get to Mission Beach midway between Cairns and Townsville (for example, by the bus service which runs once or twice a day on the coast highway) there are several water taxi companies which can take you to Dunk ($A27 for 1-5 persons). There are two launches ($A12 round trip) leaving from nearby Clump Point about six miles from Dunk by water. Reaching Dunk by way of the bus is more complex than flying, however, since it requires fairly close scheduling, a two hour bus ride from Townsville or Cairns to Tully (about $A6), taxi from Tully to Clump Point and then the forty-five minute launch to Dunk.

The resort is owned by TransAustralia Airlines (TAA), the government-owned carrier, which makes every effort to run a sophisticated and efficient operation.The staff greets guests on

THE GREAT BARRIER REEF

arrival at the island's airstrip with a complimentary glass of champagne and orange juice. Brief registration formalities are taken care of right at the terminal. Guests are greeted by name as they present their vouchers and have their names checked off the arrival list, and then are efficiently transported directly to their rooms aboard a van or small bus. Room assignments have been completed in advance so there is no delay in getting to your room and immediately into the spirit of the island. Luggage is brought along shortly by one of the porters (they're the ones wearing the shirt labeled *porter* – and they don't stand by hoping for a gratuity.)

TAA has spent more than $2.3 million on its Great Barrier Reef Hotel, with 140 well designed top-class units accommodating up to 320 guests. There are four distinct types of accommodations. **Sundeck rooms** are the lowest price ($A84 per person, double occupancy, including all meals) and are grouped in a single two-story block near the beach. **Banfield units** ($A90) are set back in tropical surroundings. **Cabana Suites** ($A100) are scattered around the central complex in a tropical garden setting. **Beachfront Cabanas** ($A120) are just off the beach and offer considerably more privacy. All of these prices include virtually all activities and facilities, except for those requiring fuel, such as power boats.

All of the rooms show attention to architectural and interior decorating detail. In the **Cabana Suites**, an entire wall is glass with a large sliding door to the terrace. The ceilings are very high (perhaps sixteen feet), and the space is ample. Open the front glass door and back door, keeping the screens closed, and the overhead circulating fan facilitates pleasant circulation of the tropical breezes. Decor is simple, with emphasis on light colors, including the floor tile and light woven mat floor cover, creating a pleasantly clean tropical effect. The bathroom facilities are modest, but quite satisfactory.

Twice-a-day housemaid service is efficient, but, as with a few other Barrier Reef resorts, you have to plead for extra towels to take to beach or pool. Go to the resort laundry, located behind the guest laundry facilities, and ask the staff for a couple of towels which they will be delighted to furnish. The drinks man restocks your room refrigerator daily and will take orders for extra sodas or specific wines from the resort's ample wine list for your room.

Life at **Dunk** is very informal. Dress up for dinner means putting on a shirt with a collar and, if shorts are worn, long socks. The large dining pavilion is open-air and nicely laid out. Light music – one day pop classics, another day *golden oldies*, is piped in during breakfast and lunch, and a pianist plays light classics during dinner.

Buffet breakfast is an exceptionally nice array of fresh fruits, cereals, juices, and a hot table with a broad selection from eggs to steak to spaghetti. Lunch is again a buffet among Barrier Reef resorts – and is generally the best meal of the day at **Dunk**. The buffet table was perfect for the tropics: fresh cold giant prawns, fish salads, a broad selection of cold meats and salads, hot table with fresh reef fish, breaded scallops and shrimp, quiche, stir fried vegetables, and meats. There was also a cheese board and large selection of fresh fruits. A drinks waiter will take your order, serving beer, wines or whatever.

During our stay, dinner, served á la carte with a choice of, three main courses (remember Australia calls the preliminary course the entrée), was somewhat uneven. Perhaps we were more critical of **Dunk** than other resorts because the dining room came so highly advertised, or perhaps the particular kitchen staff that month was not operating at peak performance. Regrettably, our dinners were not as the travel promotion literature had predicted. The first evening, the appetizer course of king prawns, served with a very light cocktail sauce, was absolutely delightful – as good as the TV commercials for Australian tourism suggest. On the other hand, the main courses generally were a little disappointing.

Coq au vin (here cooked with red wine, bacon and mushroom sauce) tasted too much of canned mushroom sauce and the chicken was less than perfect. Beef Wellington seemed a bit contrived; we felt that a simple steak would have been preferable to their presentation. The coral trout teriyaki *–a fillet of coral trout marinated in soy sauce, orange juice, ginger and spring onions, and grilled* – tasted like it was marinated only in soy sauce and grilled...and grilled...and grilled! We began to wonder if, because the resort is owned by an airline, the kitchen felt the need to serve airline food at least once a day.

There are some very distinct pluses in the dining room in the evening, however.The dining pavilion itself is a very attractive, inviting large open structure, well appointed and very pleasantly staffed. The service is pleasant and attentive. The atmosphere is very congenial and provides ample opportunities for visiting with the other guests of the resort. While by no means overly formal, there is a pleasant sophistication to the operation.

The cheese board – set up in the middle of the dining room on a serve-yourself basis – was simple but excellent. The wine list is something of which the resort can well be proud. They have fairly priced the local wines and offer a broad selection. Other visitors have had very pleasant things to say about **Dunk's** cuisine. In all likelihood the fine reputation it has in the region was earned and deserved. We certainly wouldn't discourage anyone from visiting this resort just because our dinners fell a bit short of the standards described in their brochure.

Indeed, one regular **Dunk** dining event stands out as a stellar food attraction of the entire region. Friday evening the resort features its *seafood smorgasbord* with fresh prawns, superb Queensland mud crabs (which, we reported earlier, are quite similar to San Francisco Dungeness crab), Moreton Bay bugs (those delicious baby lobsters we also mentioned earlier), sand crabs, abalone, smoked eel, reef fish and oysters, to which they add whole roast suckling pig, turkey, ham and assorted salads. The selection is excellent, definitely ample, and beautifully laid out. The kitchen staff is available at the buffet table to explain the various selections and to see that the platters are kept heaping full. It's easy to understand why many visitors bring their cameras to this affair.

A few steps opposite the dining pavilion, the open two-story high entertainment complex is a large pleasant space with comfortable and attractive seating arrangements.The tropical island style building is done in regional woods with attractive colorful fabrics. The main bar, as well as the dance floor, are situated here, and the atmosphere, both day and evening, overlooking the swimming pool and the bay beyond, is delightful and relaxing.

After dinner there is live entertainment and the resident dance band (of course calling themselves *Papillon* , after the island's abundant supply of butterflies) plays every night. Generally the music is a mix of sixties and seventies U.S. pop rock. On

THE GREAT BARRIER REEF

Saturday they have western night! There is a television lounge where a recent release afternoon movie is shown daily and Jane Fonda videotape exercise programs are run once or twice a day. For the very hungry, there is a coffee shop. There is also a hair dressing salon, baby sitting service (at normal rates other than during dinner, when they will care for children over three at no charge while you dine), conference facilities for 80, telex, and two STD pay phones. There are only telephones available to resort guests, meaning occasional lines in the evening. They are located outside the reception office.

on Dunk Island

The resort has laid out three or four pleasant walks to and around various parts of the island.These graded walks are charted on a map provided by the resort. *Pay attention to their time estimates.* It takes longer to walk about on this island than you might expect, and the forest could prove very mystifying, and even a bit frightening, if you are lost there at dusk. The stroll to the southern coast *Coconut Beach* is about a two hour round trip. Along the way you get a splendid view of islands within 5 miles. There are daily horseback riding excursions as well.

Bedarra, 3 miles away, is being developed into another tropical resort and is visited five times weekly by a boat trip/barbecue cruise from Dunk ($A20). *Timana Island,* to west of Bedarra, can technically be reached on foot at low tide (but a boat is a safer idea) from the mangrove flats at the southern end of the Dunk Island runway. It is the home of a well known Australian tapestry artist.

Fifty-minute sea plane trips to the Outer Barrier Reef ($A35) take five people for a breathtaking view of the large expanse of reef. This type of excursion may be the only way to appreciate the reef in broad perspective, even though it still only displays a relatively small portion of the grandeur of this fantastic natural structure. Day-long launch trips on the ten passenger *Avenger* ($A60, including lunch, but drinks a small charge extra) or*Gamefisher* ($A70) to the Outer Barrier Reef (weather and tides permitting, as with so many activities involving the Outer Reef) give you a chance to snorkel and fish on the very edge of the sea protected by the massive reef.

There is a pretty golf course (6-hole, except on Sunday when they commandeer one of the holes for Lord Montague Dunk

Ground, where they hold a cricket match – *Dunk's Dozen* versus *Australia*), an archery range behind the tennis courts, horseback riding on trails through the forest ($A8), cata- marans and wind surfers, water skiing (somewhat expensive at $A5 per run or $30 for half hour), clay pigeon shooting, a badminton court, volleyball, pool, ping pong, and tennis courts with a strange simulated grass/carpet surface (called *Super Grasse*) which collects blown sand, making it most interesting to try to predict the bounce. Incidentally, the resort provides tennis rackets and balls and golf clubs and carts without charge.

There are limited laundry facilities – four washing machines, dryers, irons and boards – available for resort guests without charge – and they even give you laundry soap.The machines are quite busy during the daytime, but since they are available twenty-four hours, you might consider using them later in the evening, or before an early game of tennis before breakfast.

TAA continues what, according to one writer, has become a **Dunk** tradition – *that of changing managers every few days, weeks, or months. In less than fifteen years there have been well over fifty managers.* If there is any shortcoming at **Dunk Island,** it is a perceptible lack of imagination on the part of management. For example, when we were there the resort manager and most of the executive staff left the manager's weekly welcoming party early, and were not present to greet guests who accepted the resort's invitation for cocktails. As another example, no one at the reception desk could even begin to suggest how to go about planning direct transportation to Hinchinbrook resort, situated on a massive island visible from Dunk, because evidently none of the people working behind the desk had ever visited Hinchinbrook. You should also be aware that, since the reception desk is open only at 9:00 a.m. (and not a *minute* earlier, and doors are locked until then), you must be sure to make appropriate arrangements if you have an early departure by water taxi, since all check-out activity – including baggage pick-up and transport – at this sizeable resort is geared around scheduled departures by air.

The above not withstanding, **Dunk** offers you every opportunity for a very action filled holiday in a lovely environment, at a generally very efficiently operated resort. Particularly among the larger resorts, **Dunk's** accommodations are the nicest, and its surroundings about the most inviting. It offers as much in the way of ocean centered activity as any other resort. It is very popular with families (that means lots of little kids, if that's important to you) and is a great place for an easy holiday.

Dunk Island Resort
Dunk Island
via Townsville, Qld. 4810 [70] 688 199

Reservations through TAA

platforms of coral reef near Lizard Island

FAIRFAX ISLETS

• no resort • coral cays • no tourist facilities

You may come across reference to **Fairfax** in literature about the Great Barrier Reef. It actually consists of two coral cays in the Bunker Group, south of Heron Island and below the Tropic of Capricorn. Vegetation on the windward cay was destroyed by practice bombing during World War II, representing a tragic, irreparable loss. There are *no resort or tourist facilities* on these cays.

Fitzroy Island

FITZROY

• coral viewing • bushwalks • fishing
• snorkeling • swimming

THE GREAT BARRIER REEF

This continental island in the Coral Sea, only 14 miles from Cairns and 8 miles from the Outer Barrier Reef, is circled with beaches that ring like crystal when you walk on the heavy coral gravel which has been washed up over the sand. A small, dense tropical rain forest includes eucalyptus, streams, waterfalls, wild orchids and butterflies. This is an unspoiled island with beautiful coral flats, a good deep anchorage, and ample fresh water.

There is no evidence that any aboriginal tribe inhabited Fitzroy, although it was used as a hunting ground. There is some chance that early Chinese, Japanese, and natives from New Guinea visited the island, as well as others off North Queensland, but left no discernible traces. The first sighting of Fitzroy Island by a European was Captain Cook on June 10, 1770. He named the island in honor of the Duke of Grafton, a prominent politician and illegitimate son of Charles II. Two days later, Cook's ship, the *Endeavor*, ran aground on the reef.

The abundance of fresh water made the island very attractive to subsequent nautical visitors. During the late nineteenth century there was a large Chinese migration to north Australia. Partly due to European prejudices, and partly to the threat of small pox from China, in 1877 Fitzroy was made a quarantine station for Chinese immigrants, who were required to remain there for sixteen days to test for signs of ill health. Evidently these quarantine periods were extended until officials could not detect even the slightest signs of ill health. As a result, many Chinese did not survive the quarantine and are buried on the island.

Access to Fitzroy Island is by *M.V. Fitzroy Flyer,* a high speed (28 knot) catamaran which carries 172 passengers, departing Fitzroy Marina on the Esplanade in Cairns daily at 9:00 a.m. for the 40 minute trip. The trip ($27 round trip –$20 off season–plus $13 if you want the buffet lunch and glass bottom boat trip on Fitzroy) includes an afternoon stop at Green Island. The lunch at **Fitzroy Resort** is $A10 and can be purchased after arrival. There is also an optional trip to the Outer Reef ($A17 round trip, $A19 including lunch) which takes one hour each way, but is very weather sensitive. Friday and Saturday nights the *Fitzroy Flyer* operates special schedules, returning to the mainland about midnight to allow day visitors to attend the resort's weekend entertainment. On Wednesday nights the island's stores are ferried over, so the resort operates a *booze cruise* evening round trip.

The resort currently has accommodations for a maximum of 30 overnight guests ($A75 per person per day with all meals; $A55 for the third and additional adults; children $A35) in five self-contained villas (up to 6 people accommodated in each) just off the the beach. We were told that the local government authorities plan to allow expansion of the island's facilities in the next few years, in part to alleviate the increasing congestion on nearby Green Island.

Units are very clean but relatively spartan.They have a double bed, single bunk, and a back room, which is really an enclosed porch, with a double bunk. Cabins have a private bath, color television, radio, ceiling fan, large patio, unstocked refrigerator and kitchen sink, but no serious cooking capability beyond a toaster. Laundry facilities are available.

The quite pleasant open central complex has a restaurant and bar, dive shop and souvenir stand. There is a fast-food kiosk, selling fish and chips, huge hot dogs, and the like, with a good selection of soft drinks. Friday and Saturday nights the resort features professional entertainment.

THE GREAT BARRIER REEF

Lunch is a fixed price ($A10) affair. On our first visit it was a beautiful cold smorgasbord spread.Our favorites were the cold roast chicken and cold steamed baramundi, served with a slice of pineapple and a traditional selection of sauces. The choice of cold cuts and salads was quite satisfactory. Fresh cold vegetables and fruit set off the table nicely. By our second visit, the smorgasbord had been abandoned in favor of a barbecue, which offered a selection of meats done on the grill while you waited and was quite nice.There was a pleasant selection of salads and other accompaniments.

Feel free to take your plate outside and sit on the terrace overlooking the bay for the best table in town. The bar stocks, at quite moderate prices, a rather good selection of Australian wines and several varieties of beers.

You can view the coral from a glass-bottom boat for an hour each day at 11:00 a.m.; explore the island using one of the well marked walking tracks through the rain forest, to the light house or the butterfly glen. There is a new semi-submersible, one of the new breed of motorized barges with a large underwater bubble.This one seats about 25 people ($A10) for a lovely cruise around the island's reef. Underwater, the bay contains 300 varieties of live coral. Swarming shoals of small fish have been tamed by twice daily tropical fish feeding from the jetty. The resort also has paddle skiing (glass panel skis available), fishing, canoeing, water bikes – *even a nudey beach* says the brochure. Lie on the beach, snorkel or just relax in a paddle boat. There is no swimming pool, however.In 1984 the government es-tablished a *breeding station for the giant sea clams,* which have become nearly extinct in the vicinity because of over-fishing by Taiwanese poachers. The poachers find a large market for the clams in China, where they are considered to possess aphrodisiac properties. Regrettably, the operators charge to view the rather nondescript clam facility, which consists of a few large concrete vats. You can just as easily peek over the fence. According to a marine biologist who works there, it takes about 15 months to raise a clam large enough to be sold commercially or deposited on the reef, ultimately to grow to 10 kilograms of bivalve or larger.

We enjoyed our brief sojourns to Fitzroy. It is an easy and pleasant day trip from Cairns, and the Flyer makes a nice introduction to the Barrier Reef world if you enter through that Gateway and have time to spare. Fitzroy could also offer a *very quiet, very secluded resort vacation,* but the quietude and limited activity schedule would suggest only a brief holiday unless total relaxation is your goal.

Fitzroy Island
P.O. Box 2120
Cairns, Qld. 4870

[70] 557 118
Reservations through Fitzroy Island, cc/o Tourist Booking Office, Marlin Parade, Cairns, Qld. 4870; telephone [70] 515 477

on Fitzroy Island

Lizard Island

FRASER

- bushwalks • fishing • snorkeling
- swimming • camping

Magnetic Is.
Flinders Passage
C. Bowling Green
TOWNSVILLE
PORT DENISON
Bowen
Cumberland Islands
REPULSE BAY
Pompey Reefs
MACKAY
Prudhoe Is.
Swain Reefs
Northumberland Islands
BROAD SOUND
CAPRICORN CHANNEL
ROCKHAMPTON
Curtis Is.
CAPRICORN GROUP
BUNKER GROUP
GLADSTONE
PORT CURTIS
Lady Elliot Is
Fraser Island
BRISBANE

CAIRNS
The Great Barrier Reef
TOWNSVILLE
MACKAY
ROCKHAMPTON
QUEENSLAND
BRISBANE

THE GREAT BARRIER REEF

This is the largest sandy island in the world, and is located approximately 150 miles north-east of Brisbane. The sand which makes up the island is not from the region, but instead the sea has carried it from the south until it piled up against undersea obstacles. The dense plant life which has developed prevents the giant island from being washed away. A great deal of political controversy surrounded the island during the 1970's, when Australia's strong conservationist movement succeeded in having the federal government declare a ban on timber and sand mining operations on Fraser.

Fraser Island is not truly part of the Great Barrier Reef region, since it is well south of the southern extent of the reef itself. It is geographically close, however, and advertises in many of the same publications that promote Barrier Reef holidays. If you are travelling north from Brisbane, it could be along the way.

Here you find wilderness, freshwater lakes, rocky headlands and forests. Part of the island is a national park. Because of its sub-tropical location, Fraser combines tropical and temperate with birds and fish of both climates. There are dense rain forests with abundant wildlife. The most prominent features of the island are *towering sand dunes* as high as 750 feet above sea level, *Woongoolbver Creek* with its sandy bottom and canopy of palms, ferns and vines, *Lake Wabby* (its deepest lake) and numerous other lakes. Fraser is advertised as *a geologist's fantasy, a naturalist's workshop and in parts, a scenic imperative* and it boasts a coastline of almost 200 miles.

It is difficult and challenging to explore this island, however. The terrain is a series of sharply defined sand dunes which have been characterized as an endless repetition of ridges. These peaks are very close together, so one would be climbing constantly and descending sand hills. Add to this the thickness of the vegetation, and you have a real wilderness adventure. The island is criss-crossed with forestry tracks suitable for four-wheel-drive vehicles, but at the very least these are a real navigational challenge. Should you desire to undertake this test, you must obtain a *permit* to leave the shore areas. Consult the Duty Ranger on the island or the National Park and Wildlife Service in Brisbane for visiting permits, and the District Forester in Maryborough for driving permits.

Fraser Island is reached by one hour flight from Brisbane via Nomad Airways or Barrier Reed Airways (approximately $A60 each way for the thirty minute flights) or Orchid Beach Air Service from Maryborough (daily except Tuesday and Thursday, thirty minutes, $A70 per person round trip) [telephone Orchid Beach 2]. Charter flights are available ($A100/hour for a 5-seat aircraft and $A180/hour for a 9 seat) from Whittakers Air Services in Maryborough [telephone (071) 22 2255]. There is also car ferry service from either Inskip Point on the mainland to Hook Point (daily between 6:30 a.m. and 4:00 p.m., ten minute trip, $A30-32 per vehicle) or Bullock Point on the island; or Urangan on the coast to Moon Point or Urang Creek; or River Heads to Deep Creek. The barge landing is 67 miles from Orchid Beach.

Orchid Beach Island Village ($A50 per person, meals included), overlooking Marloo Bay, is a Polynesian-style resort with twenty-five cabins with shower and fan, licensed dining room, pool, tennis court, fishing, water skiing, and evening entertainment.

At happy Valley, about 30 miles north of Inskip Point, **Beacon Lodge Holiday Flats** [telephone Happy Valley 4U] has a self-contained flat which will accommodate six persons ($A22/day for two persons; $A130/week). **Boom Crest** [telephone (071) 82 2522] has two flats for 1-6 persons ($A28/day; $A160-180/week, linen rental extra). **Elanora** [telephone Happy Valley 1] also has two flats fro 1-6 persons ($A26-40/day; $A150-180/week, linen rental extra). **Fraser Lodge** and **Fraser Unit** [telephone Happy Valley 6K] each have one flat accommodating 8 ($A26-30/day; $A130-180/week, linen extra). **Fraser Sands** has two flats accommodating

on Dunk Island

six persons ($A28-30/day; $A160 180/week). **Happy Valley Resort** [telephone Happy Valley 1] has six flats accommodating 6 persons ($A24 30/day; $A110-160/week). **Murava House** [telephone (071) 82 3447] has one flat for six persons ($A24 30/day; $A150-180/week).

Eurong Beach Resort [telephone Ungowa 7U] offers a choice between the resort and lodge style accommodations. There are 35 units accommodating up to 8 persons, some with fans, radio, coffee and tea makers, refrigerators and cooking facilities ($A35 per day per person with all meals; $A135-185/week for 1-8 persons without meals.) There are general stores at **Eurong Beach Tourist Resort** and **Happy Valley**. There is a National Fitness Camp at Dilli Village, 5 miles south of Eurong.

Cruise tours are available to Fraser on the *Fraser Princess* and *M.V. Philanderer* out of Urangan.

For further information contact Queensland Tourist and Travel Corp., 3550 Wilshire Boulevard, Los Angeles, California 90010; telephone (213) 381-3062, or Hervy Bay Town Council, corner Bideford and Campbell Streets, Torquay, Qld. 4657; telephone (071) 28 2855.

on Great Keppel Island

GREAT KEPPEL

- coral viewing • national park • bushwalks
- fishing • waterskiing • anchorage
- tennis • sailing • snorkeling • windsurfing
- swimming • camping

THE GREAT BARRIER REEF

The perfect place for a tropical suntan, making friends and dancing the night away, says one Aussie tourist bureau promotion piece. Great Keppel Island lies just inside the Tropic of Capricorn, 30 to 35 miles northeast of Rockhampton, eight miles off the coast. It was also the largest of the group of Barrier Reef islands named by Captain Cook. Once a sheep station, the old homestead is intact on the mountain.There are also private homes on the island near the resort. It is one of the larger resort islands and is gifted with *seventeen sandy white beaches* covering 17 miles. This island claims to have more sunshine than any other area off the East Coast of Australia. It is 24 miles from the nearest point on the outer Great Barrier Reef.

Great Keppel is reached by most resorts guests by means of the 15 to 20 minute flight from Rockhampton on Sunstate Airlines 20-passenger *DeHavilland Twin Otter* ($A75.40 round trip; price included in packages). It is a beautiful short flight, giving you a chance to see the coastal region where some of Australia's best beef is raised, the Fitzroy river, pineapple plantations, some mangrove swamps, and the coastal beach town of Rosslyn Bay and Yeppoon. Although there is a daily launch ($A14 round trip) – and talk of a four-day-a-week hydrofoil which we never saw ($A18 round trip) – from Rosslyn Bay Boat Harbor via Yeppoon approximately 43 miles north of Rockhampton, getting from *Rocky* airport to the wharf may prove tricky so most visitors from outside of North Queensland arrive by air.

There is a somewhat open but adequate anchorage, and there are many nearby islands which make the idea of chartering a boat for a few days to see Great Keppel and its surroundings a pleasant prospect for qualified sailors. You can check local listings, which you can pick up at the Rockhampton airport, for boat and yacht rental agencies.

Much of Great Keppel is national park. Some small portions are privately owned fee interests where there are private residences. The balance of the island, including the entire resort, is located on an old grazing leasehold which was purchased outright in the mid-1970's by TransAustralia Airlines (TAA), which also owns and operates Dunk Island several hundred miles to the north. **Great Keppel Resort,** located at Fishermans Beach, has 140 rather undistinguished motel type units with accommodations for as many as 350 guests; 20 new units will increase the resort capacity to over 400 in August 1985.

Three types of accommodations are offered – older single-story standard or *garden* bungalows ($A75 per person per day, double occupancy, including all meals; $A68 per night for stays of seven nights or more), smaller, but newer garden units, in a large two story L-shaped blockhouse facing the tennis courts (same prices), and the same smaller units in a block house facing the water and called Beachfront units ($A79, reduced to $A71 for more than a week).There were formerly several units described as *deluxe,* which are considerably larger than the other beach front rooms. The expansion program, however, has cut off the beach view from these rooms, so they have been down-classified and will rent as beachfront, without view. These, in fact ,are probably the superior accommodations in the resort, with small tub and shower as well as balconies or verandas. There are two super-deluxe suites at $A250 per day, but these are not in the reservations computer and are held principally for visiting VIPs.

Speaking of the computer, the whole operation at **Great Keppel** is apparently conducted out of TAA's central offices, connected electronically with the resort. As a result, the resort cannot give credits or make financial adjustments, and any refunds must come out of Brisbane.

The resort's rooms need refurbishing and remodelling, but unfortunately the current $A3 million expansion program evidently does not call for that. Units have chartreuse chenille bedspreads and industrial indoor-outdoor carpeting. The walls in the single-story bungalow units are insufficiently adorned painted clapboard, and the balance of the rooms are painted cinderblock with gunnite ceilings. Facilities include private shower and toilet in plain utilitarian bathrooms, ceiling fan, unstocked refrigerator, tea and coffee making facilities. There are no dressers or proper vanities. Lighting is poor.

Ventilation in the older regular units is primitive and poor. The overhead fan circulates the air, but there are insufficient windows and doors for cross- ventilation, so the rooms remain quite warm – five to ten degrees warmer, in fact, than the outside tropical world. The beachfront and newer garden units are considerably smaller than the *family* apartments, and are situated in ranks of two story block houses, but it is possible to open the entrance door at one end ,and sliding glass doors at the other to catch any breezes.

Meals are served in the *Admiral Keppel* dining room. Great Keppel Island was named after this First Lord of the Admiralty by Captain Cook. We are told that the Admiral never set foot on the island and, never having married, left no descendants. It was all right that the resort tried to imitate the interior of an old sailing ship, (they have hooked the ceiling lanterns up so they cutely sway uniformly from side to side through dinner, but, thank goodness, not at breakfast and lunch as well) but the industrial white plastic ceiling quickly breaks the spell, and the well worn indoor-outdoor carpet with random plank wood stenciled on it is too much. And we truly doubt that any ship's galley was ever crowded with formica tables and stackable chairs.

We were promised by the promotional literature that breakfasts offered unlimited fruit juice, eggs, bacon, sausages, fruit, tea or coffee. This is true as far as it goes, but what it really describes is an unattractive buffet where no one pays much attention to the appearance of the food, which has been dumped unceremoniously on serving platters. The hot table is adequate, but the cold fruit selection is not for an island resort.

Lunch promised *a mountainous smorgasbord of hot and cold dishes,* seafood, fruit, salads, cold meats.Translated, this became a few cold cuts, no cold fish and no cheeses, a very small selection of salad materials, and mediocre hot foods. Luncheon beverages are also entirely self-service.

Dinner was of the same quality. The soup course – seafood chowder, oxtail, tomato – with only one type (no choices) each evening is followed by one entrée (again no choices) such as overly breaded frozen prawns or, another night, an avocado vinaigrette which was actually rather good. The main courses were quite uneven. One evening the fish was fresh and flavorful; the next it was bland and drowned in a thick commercial sauce. The chicken oriental (soy sauce, on a bed of rice) was quite fine, but the beef iwasaki (soy sauce, pineapple and ginger) was poor. Desserts are generally unimaginative, although, to be fair, the apple pie, when offered was very enjoyable, and the pleasant staff told us we could always just request plain ice cream, which was fairly good. A very small, thoroughly uninspired, but inexpensive wine list, with the bulk of the offerings in the $A8-12 range, provided appropriate accompaniment to the food.

Friday is *Island Night* : a buffet *under the stars* including seafood, cold cuts, salads, fruits and cheeses. Sound familiar ? larger lunch plus fish? Right, but scratch dessert. It was not offered with this particular dinner. The addition of Moreton Bay bugs (those exquisite midget lobsters they get in Queensland) was nice, and the very nice woman serving them – these they don't let you help yourself to – gave us each *one,* which is like being given one big prawn. The chilled mud crab, another Queensland specialty, was left on a platter so guests could serve themselves a more generous portion.

To compound matters, the Friday buffet dinner is served around the rectangular swimming pool outside the dining room and is very poorly organized, so that it can only be approached on one side of the tables. Moreover, there is only one platter of each item. The result is that you have to be prepared for a very long line until just before dinner ends at 8:00. We would have to say this was about the least impressive buffet we found anywhere among Barrier Reef resorts.

There are programmed night time activities generally beginning by 10:30 p.m. and going on until every one reaches exhaustion. Six nights a week the resident rock group livens up the *Wreck Bar* until approximately 2:00 a.m., and the crowds remain rambunctious until 3:00 a.m. or 4:00 a.m. This can make the standard rooms at the back of the resort a blessing in disguise. *The Sand Bar*, adjacent to the to the dining room, is supposed to be *quieter* in the evening, but it didn't seem noticeably so since every night was cabaret night. Even floor shows and dress-up nights were loud and the crowd boisterous.

This is a beautiful island blessed with natural adaptation for water sports and sightseeing. Regrettably, the **Great Keppel** resort is not operated to take advantage of this bounty. First of all, when we asked at reception whether there are day trips by plane or boat to the Outer Barrier Reef, we were told that *the reef is 50 miles away* (actually it's more like thirty miles), so there is no activity involving the main reef. In fact, in this, the staff also was in error, since we found that one independent charterer on the island does offer expensive catamaran service to the Outer Reef for $A800, carrying 15 or 16 passengers on a day trip. This, therefore, is probably *the only Barrier Reef resort in Australia which practically ignores the Barrier Reef.* Local Rockhampton and Yeppoon promotional literature suggests that you could probably charter planes or boats along the coast to pick you up on the island and take you to the reef and back. We feel it is wrong, however, that the visitor is required to be on his or her own devices with no Outer Reef activity easily available through the resort.

There are many local water activities handled on the beach through the resort's *Keppel Kuatics,* including ,without charge, large two-passenger water tricycles (on which two of you can pedal across the top of the bay), one and two passenger paddle boards, wind surfing, 13' catamarans, and brief coral viewing and snorkeling trips. There is a charge for paraflying and water skiing on days when these activities are offered. For a small charge, they will also deliver you and pick you up by motorboat so you can enjoy any number of very beautiful long sand beaches on the island. You can also hire one of their motor boats for 2, 4 or 6 hours between 9:00 a.m. and 4:00 p.m..

There is also a very pleasant charter yacht, the *Binda,* available on some days for half-day snorkel and fishing excursions ($A20 per person) or charter ($A200 for the boat for a full day). This is an independent operation and not offered through the resort.

THE GREAT BARRIER REEF

Even though it departs from *Keppel Kuatics,* you must take some money to pay the skipper directly, since you cannot charge the price to your room. Hidden around the sand spit ,about a half-mile to the north of the hotel ,is an independent dive shop which also offers short scuba and snorkel excursions via power boat. They reduce their price if you bring your own gear or the snorkel equipment which the resort will lend you. Scuba divers can refill their tanks here also.

There are also regular boat connections from off the beach, just past *Keppel Kuatics ,* to the underwater observatory (admission $A5) on the adjacent island. The resort promotes a free daily morning *Booze Krooze* , which sails around the island with an optional stop at the observatory, and there is an old ferry which plies back and forth from the beach to the observatory every forty-five minutes or so. This observatory, the largest of its kind in Australia, faces the fringing reef on one side, and a sunken Taiwanese junk on the other. It offers a chance to view the mid-size fish feeding at the reef and quite large fish living in the sunken wreck.

Away from the beach, the resort has two in adequately maintained asphalt tennis courts and an adjacent brand new one. There are archery sessions, cricket matches, volleyball, ping pong, excellent bush walks around the island, and well organized activities for the younger children. It quickly becomes apparent that one of the most favored activities of resort visitors is drinking at the circular bar at the large *Peanut Pool* .

The resort has a snack bar (the *Keppel Kafe*), limited island shop, hairdressing salon, baby sitting for under three year olds arranged through reception, photographer (the *Keppel*

Klicker), laundry facilities, telex and bank available in the reception office and two or three STD pay phones scattered around the resorts (expect lines in the evening).

Keppel's brochures pitch to a party crowd, and it works. The resort enjoys roughly 95% occupancy year round, with a heavy

landing on Great Keppel Island

THE GREAT BARRIER REEF

concentration of Melbournean youth [over 60% of the patrons are under 35] and vacationers attracted by the cheap air fares and package deals. For seven years, their motto on their posters and stenciled on the tee shirts invited us to *Get wrecked at Great Keppel* . The assistant manager assured us that the new ad campaign referred to the abundant athletic activities which the resort offers. The new brochure, however, features pictures of a smiling topless girl, whom we are assured in the ad is but nineteen years old. To avoid any suggestion of chauvinism, there is also a suggestive photo of three girls pulling the trunks from a partially obscured, but obviously male guest. Their ad continues,

> *something in the island air makes people's inhibitions drop faster than Newton's apples. Nothing will prepare you for the Keppel Sexual Olympics. Still, Aussie girls are getting a reputation for stamina events, and this could be your chance to prove it's all true. ....The indoor marathon and relay are popular events (but only for the fit and dedicated).*

Actually, whatever went on behind closed doors, there was much less topless sunbathing here than at other resorts, such as Hamilton Island, and little suggestion of promiscuity. The kids - and that's in reality what most of them really were, albeit some of them rather older *kids* - wore tee shirts with scatological exaggerations stenciled on them, but in the evening donned some of their nicest clothes for dinner.In contrast to the easy sexual theme of the brochures, there is even a dress code in the *Wreck Bar*. The biggest adventure for many of the young hotel guests seems to be ordering fancy tropical drinks or stacking empty beer cans next to the swimming pool.

The sad part about this operation is that it would have been a better Kings Cross nightclub in Sydney or suburban Brisbane resort –perhaps at *Surfers Paradise* – without wasting such a beautiful island. Sorry Wreckers, **Keppel** may be *Kute* , but in our book it can't hold a Kandle to TAA's other resort, **Dunk Island**. We really couldn't see much reason why Americans should go so far out of their way to visit this island, unless the travel opportunities are somehow irresistible or circumstances restrict you to within fifty miles of Rockhampton.

Great Keppel Island
P.O. Box 108
Rockhampton, Qld. 4700

[79] 391 744
Reservations through TAA

Green   Island

GREEN

- coral viewing • national park • bushwalks
- scuba diving • snorkeling • swimming

THE GREAT BARRIER REEF

This island was sighted, but not visited, in 1770 by Captain Cook, who named it after the *Endeavor's* astronomer, Charles Green. Coconuts were planted on the island a century ago to provide food for shipwrecked sailors. It was first served commercially in 1899 by the Butler family, who established a ferry connection. The resort is now owned and operated by the Hayles family, which runs most of the boats which service the island regularly from Cairns.

Green is a true coral cay, composed entirely of pulverized coral washed up by tide and wave action. A very small sand island, Green is roughly two miles long by one mile wide and rises only about ten feet above sea level. As you approach, it looks every bit the prototype palm-crowned desert island of every adventure story ever filmed. Located 16 miles (or so, depending which government travel brochure you read) from Cairns, it is a popular day-visit resort for Northern Queensland. Perched right on the Great Barrier Reed, Green is an excellent spot for snorkeling and , because the reef shelf drops away offshore, for scuba diving.

Green island is one of a tiny number of developed islands located on the Barrier Reef itself. Heron Island is the only other resort island undeniably on the reef. Lizard Island claims to be part of the reef and is probably close enough to being a true reef island to qualify, but it is a granite continental island and not a true coral cay. Lady Elliot is on the reef, but has only camping cabins and no true developed resort. The balance of the islands are situated well inside the Outer Barrier Reef.

Classified as a national park, all plants, wildlife, fish and shells on and around Green are protected. The entire island is covered with a mass of trees and light vegetation growing to within a few yards of the shore line. The beaches are white sand.

The island is easily reached by several cruise companies on regular service during the mornings from the Esplanade in Cairns. Large launches carrying up to 250 people ($A11.50 round trip), for example, leave at 9:00 a.m. and return at 3:15 arriving back at Cairns at 4:30. A faster service, *Hayles Green Island Express* ($A19.50 round trip), departs Hayles wharf daily at 8:30 and 10:30 for a forty minute trip, returning at 2:30 and 4:30. From Marlin Wharf *Cruise Center* jetty, the 75' twin-hull *Coral Seatel* ($A12 round-trip, including lunch, coral viewing, and some admissions to island attractions), carrying 160 people daily, departs Cairns at 9:00 a.m. and returns at 5:00 p.m.

The **Underwater Observatory** established in 1954 is the biggest advertised attraction of Green Island, and is probably its biggest single disappointment. It is a large 70-ton sunken steel chamber with 22 portholes. In truth, this is just a big steel tube sunk in 15 or 20 feet of sea with clams, coral and sea life *imported* into the area. On the surface, outside the gadget and souvenir shop, are plainly identified *replicas* of anchors and other debris from wrecks in the area. If you enjoy snorkeling, save $3 and, weather and tide permitting, follow the clearly marked underwater trail laid out for swimming around the observatory in water about 14 feet deep, but hugging the jetty and observatory.

If you liked the observatory, then the next stop should probably be **Marineland Melanesia**, described in promotional literature as *a unique blend of many major zoological exhibits covering half an acre in doors and out. It houses a world renowned collection of primitive art, along with some*

THE GREAT BARRIER REEF

magnificent species of salt water crocodiles from the Papua New Guinea region. The adjacent *Barrier Reef Theater* is an exhibit which tells the life story of Noel Monkman (one of earliest pioneers on the Great Barrier Reef) and also shows films on Barrier Reef subjects.

Low tide exposes miles of the Barrier Reef for exploration. *This chance to explore the reef up close is a good reason for making a special trip to Green Island.* The opportunity to walk on the reef will depend, however, on weather and tides. If you are planning a day trip to the island, check and make sure the reef will be exposed and accessible that day. Even if wind or tide prevent your walk on the reef, you can expect a pleasant day on a lovely, if crowded, sandy beach well worth the trip if you are in Cairns and have a day to spend seeing a Great Barrier Reef island. It takes about twenty minutes to walk around the island. The forest is beautiful and full of bird life. You can swim in waters protected by reefs.

Hayles also operates the **Coral Cay Hotel** on the island offering *very* modest - a la 1930's U.S. motel cabins - small *air-conditioned bungalows* and lodge accommodations with dining room for 100 guests ($A50- 75 per person per day full board, $A39-60 m.a.p.). Adjacent *Palm Units* ($A39-45) are for lower budget guests. They are furnished with double bunks, and have air-conditioning, wardrobe and hand basin, with separate rest room facilities behind the units. Not all rooms are screened, however, with some relying on mosquito netting. Accommodations are somewhat primitive, and not for the comfort oriented. Rooms are small, and not particularly well serviced.

For guests and day trippers, the central complex of the island contains bars, a souvenir shop, bank, postal facilities, and take-out food service. Meals are rather limited, usually cold at lunch. There is a glass bottom boat service and other facilities to permit enjoying the reef area. There are day cruises available, snorkel gear at the dive shop, water skiing, but no swimming pool. Tank refills and some diving gear are available at the dive shop.

At least one commercial resort reviewer has advised travelers to skip Green or to make it a day trip only. It is criticized for being over- commercialized even by Australian standards. Nonetheless, if you enjoy the prospect of a true tropical island and only have limited time in the Cairns area, Green is well worth the easy day trip.

To combine a short visit to Green with another resort island, consider the *Fitzroy Flyer* which departs from the Esplanade marina in Cairns early in the morning, spends the morning hours and lunch at Fitzroy and makes a two hour side trip to Green before departing for Cairns at 4:15.

Coral Cay Hotel
Green Island, Qld. 4871
[70] 514 644
Reservations direct to the resort

Hamilton Island

HAMILTON

- coral viewing • bushwalks • fishing • golf
- scuba diving • anchorage • tennis • sailing
- snorkeling • windsurfing • swimming

THE GREAT BARRIER REEF

Controversial Australian entrepreneur, promoter and developer (and one-time bicycle mechanic) Keith Williams, who recently sold his Seaworld on the eastern Gold Coast reportedly for more than $A35 million, is arranging this large island to his own satisfaction. He made this possible by acquiring the complete leasehold of Hamilton Island, until ten years or so ago unspoiled and uninhabited.This fairly large resort island, though relatively dwarfed by Whitsunday and Hook Islands, its near neighbors to the north, is situated adjacent to the south coast of huge Whitsunday Island and 10 miles south-east of Shute Harbor.Without doubt, this is the most controversial island resort of the Whitsunday, in fact in Queensland, and maybe internationally, at the moment.

This very new resort (official grand opening December 8, 1984, although operating for several months before then) is entirely Keith Williams' brain-child. Having leased the island originally to establish a deer farm, Williams, after the death of his original business partner, began constructing the resort.For some reason, Australia's usually vocal conservationists remained relatively silent while Williams dynamited the top off the island's tallest peak to make it a helicopter landing site, dredged out a modern boat harbor and marina, filled in the entrance to one of the larger bays, undertook construction of a huge crushed rock seawall (because low tide otherwise left Catseye beach without adequate salt water swimming capability for several hours a day), blew the side off one of Hamilton's hills to extend the runway of his airport so jets could land (making this the only Great Barrier Reef island currently able to handle jets. Hamilton can handle small and mid-sized jets up to the new Boeing 767), and started building mid- and high-rise condominiums.

Williams sells his condos *before* construction commences. The already completed condos sold at prices ranging from $A140,000 to $A250,000, with units in the first 14-story highrise beginning at $A176,000 and increasing $1000 per floor. The latest 17-story building, which will go up in a year or two on top of one of Hamilton's hills, will have one luxury unit per floor and is already entirely sold with prices starting at $A750,000. News stories reported that former Beattle George Harrison has acquired five acres of beach on Hamilton for something in the range of $A750,000 and intends to build a private retreat there.

Plans call for several more condominium buildings, an entire small town for staff with schools for their children and shopping facilities for their families, more than a dozen restaurants, including take-out food stands, and a maximum guest population anywhere from three to five thousand people. Williams' own palatial home – with private helicopter pad, enough interior marble to outfit several churches, a basement pistol shooting range – is very prominent on the bluff above the resort. Rumor has it that after several years of construction it has yet to be completed to the owner's satisfaction.

Ansett Airlines, owner of nearby *Royal Hayman* resort, is a major investor in Hamilton Island, which perhaps helps explain why only Ansett and not TAA provides direct jet air service with Boeing 737s and 767s from Melbourne, Sydney and Brisbane Wednesday, Saturday and Sunday. Be careful of the travel literature: these flights are sometimes described as daily, except Saturday, at 10:00 a.m. and 2:00 p.m., but currently this is only projected and not yet operative.

The more likely access route for American visitors at present is through one of the nearby gateways. Hamilton is served by Air Queensland from Mackay (25 minutes, $A50 one way); from Proserpine (10 minutes, $A30 one way); via Air Whitsunday from Townsville ($A98 one way) daily except Monday and Thursday. Ansett does not yet operate non-stop service from Cairns, Townsville or any North Queensland gateway.

Hamilton Airways, the fledgling local carrier created both for charter and flight-seeing, is expanding its services to the mainland and might just gradually displace these other local carriers. They already operate from the resort with regular and charter service to Shute Harbor, Proserpine ($A30 for scheduled service), Mackay ($A50) and Townsville ($A98) by Cesna light aircraft or even Citation II executive jet. There is a full service travel agency at the resort, with a resident Ansett representative. Currently there is not enough jet traffic to have a traffic controller for their control tower reside on the island, so they fly one over from the mainland each time they have an in-coming or out-going commercial jet flight. As the population of the island increases, the controller eventually is to become a resident too.

Luxury catamarans - the *Hamilton Quick Cat* and *Hamilton Big Cat* - provide rapid connection from Shute Harbor ten miles away by water. Transit is free for guests staying at the resort. There are also day trips from Shute to Hamilton ($A25) via the *Quick Cat*. As a result of Williams' large-scale remodelling, the island boasts an excellent, but very expensive anchorage, with a floating marina which ultimately will provide berths for 400 yachts.

The Outrigger Resort, the first resort to be built (Williams has plans for a second, Mediterranean style resort on a different beach), overlooks Catseye Beach and includes fifty bungalows – prefabricated wood cabins with metal roofs; a bland exterior three-story block of luxury resort suites; mid- and high-rise condominium apartments leased back to the management concern for operation as hotel and resort facilities. As of March 1985, **Hamilton,** almost uniquely among Barrier Reef resorts, had shifted to *separate charges for accommodations and meals* and had abandoned the full board inclusive fare. Note that Hamilton charges extra for children – $A40 - $A62.50 for the first child in the room or suite, slightly lower for each additional.

Outrigger's accommodations are a study in contradiction. From the exterior one expects little, yet the interiors are as elegant as the outside is drab. Free-standing Polynesian style bures and hotel rooms in the four story **Alamanda Lodge** (both $A65 per day per person, double occupancy) or beachfront suites in the **Bougainvillaea Lodge** ($A80) and fully self-contained condominium apartments ($A160 per day for 1 bedroom, $A240 per day for 2 bedroom) are truly luxuriously appointed in contrast to other Barrier Reef resorts.

Each bure and hotel suite features king size and single bed (two queen beds in the beachfront **Bougainvillaea Lodge**), comfortable conversation area, both ceiling fans and air-conditioning, attractive rattan and wood corner bar with bar sink, glassware, and fully stocked bar refrigerator, extremely well decorated spacious bathrooms (a few of the earlier bures with shower over tub, but most with huge tile showers and double sinks, all with wall-mounted electric hair dryers and an ample supply of fine toiletries), radio, color TV, direct dial ISD and STD phones, and a small veranda or patio. Condominium apartments have one or more bedrooms, full kitchen, washers and dryers, and all of the other appointments of the hotel rooms. There are also guest laundry facilities in each building.

This is easily the largest and most nicely appointed among Great Barrier Reef resorts. Interiors are very well decorated -- attractive grass cloth walls, excellent tile work, nice interior wood. And nobody seems to care that the exterior architecture is rather tasteless by contemporary standards or that severe highrise buildings will stick out too obviously and be visible from other islands in the area for miles around, with little hope that landscaping will conceal these fundamentally unattractive buildings.

The harbor is situated across the island from the resort and is already one of the finest in North Queensland with berths for 100 boats (to be expanded to 400). For arriving yachts, mooring is $A20 for the day, $A80 for overnight. Hamilton Island is also base for a charter operation offering attractive modern yachts 40' and up and motor cruisers, available for bareboat or crewed charter for overnight or extended rental.Guests chartering boats from Hamilton are also given the use of golf carts to get around the resort while in port.

Mariner's Inn at the marina includes a restaurant, bar and disco night club upstairs, and downstairs the casual and thoroughly enjoyable *Barefoot Bar*, a jumping tavern serving snacks as well as a full range of refreshment and jammed with resort guests and *boaties*. There is also a general store downstairs selling food supplies, soft drinks, sundries, and an outdoor eating area. Across the road *Trader Pete's* sells souvenirs, casual clothing and beach gear, magazines, books, hats and post cards. An incredible amount of new construction is going on around the marina, with buildings to house the dive shop and more restaurants already substantially completed.

There still is a deer farm on the island, and Williams has added a small, if rather dismal zoo – a *fauna park* ($A2 per person; free if you buy the $A7 van tour of the resort) – which now has the animals in rather unattractive enclosures. There are four sleepy koalas in a small cinderblock structure, and a smattering of emus, peacocks, wallabies, kangaroos and a wallaroo in a fenced enclosure. The zoo is quite distant from the resort itself, so be prepared for quite a hike if you undertake to walk. The only thing we found to commend the trip, either on foot or by car, were the fine views of the Whitsunday Group from the heights of Hamilton.

Back at the resort, you will find the public rooms – the lobby, reception, bar and dining room – to be particularly attractive. Very high ceilings, split levels, thoughtful attention to decor, and skillful use of tropical woods mixed with tiles and fabrics create an elegant and very comfortable structure. Four captive dolphins live in an adjacent pool. The main resort also includes an arcade of very attractive stores, including some rather elegant up-scale offerings.

There are already several restaurants and food outlets on Hamilton. For resort guests, breakfast is in the main dining area and is what they call *continental* ($A5, includes a variety of fresh fruits, toast, sweet rolls, juices and coffee or tea) or complete ($A7.50, if you want to add the hot table offerings of eggs and meats). There is also a small adjacent *coffee shop* with á la carte selections continuously from 10 a.m. until 10 p.m.

Lunch ($A12.50) is available at the *Beach Bar and Grill* next to the swimming pool with selections such as grilled steaks, chicken, and other choices varied daily and includes an ample salad bar. The restaurant upstairs at the *Mariner's Inn*, however, offers almost identical fare as the large lunch (fixed $A10) with a less elegant salad bar. From 10 a.m.until 6 p.m. the *Beach Bar* also offers sandwiches and snacks.

Dinner is currently available at the *Dolphin Room*, the *Mariner Inn* or the *Outrigger Room*, a very satisfactory (albeit probably because of its newness, slightly uneven) seafood restaurant. In spite of its inconsistencies, we definitely preferred the *Outrigger Room*. The restaurant uses overhead fans for air circulation and is a pleasant tropical wood room with understated decor and good spacing between tables. Service is eager and friendly.

There is a broad selection of fresh fish dishes ($A12.50-$A24). The cold Queensland mud crab (seasonal prices, $A23 this evening) was very good, presented beautifully, with a good selection of sauces. The whole fresh broiled crayfish ($A24) was excellent one evening, particularly with garlic butter. The seafood pasta ($A9.50 as an entrée, $A14.50 as a main course) was frankly disappointing. Unfortunately, we found many Australian restaurants without sufficient appreciation for proper preparation of pasta.

The *Outrigger Room's* introductory courses ($A8.50-10.50) suffer a bit. The garlic prawns ($A10.50) which should have been outstanding, as they were most other places in North Queensland, were only fair. Unless you have the rabbit munchies, forget the tossed salads ($A2.50), which were unimaginative.

Wines from the medium sized, but well balanced list (emphasizing the $A15-18 range), were slightly expensive by Australian standards, and the wine waiters persist in wanting to fill your glass to the rim which just makes for warm wine in the tropics. Dinner, not including wine, will probably run $A30-40 per person with starters (other than the two $A7.50 soups), main course and desserts. This restaurant has a delicious menu. With time and closer attention in the kitchen, we hope it proves to be far more consistent. It definitely has promise.

The *Dolphin Room,* the resort's central main dining area, is far more elegant with its very high ceilings and completely open sides. It offers a very traditional menu with three different steak presentations, one fish dish, two chicken, and so forth. We suggest you avoid the beef curry ($A13.50) and stick with the simpler offerings. The New York Cut Sirloin ($A13.50) was just fine. If you inquire about the venison ($17.50) you will get conflicting stories as to whether its fresh or frozen and whether or not it is from on the island or imported. The restaurant offers a large dessert menu ($A5.50-6.75), but the most distinctive thing about it is that it tells us Macadamia nuts are also native to Queensland where they make a pleasant ice cream with them.

Food is not yet the strong suit for this resort, but we sensed that it could well improve quickly depending upon the degree of attention and supervision put into the kitchens. We also detected another, more serious shortcoming, however. Hamilton Island has grown faster than its *bore* water (well water) supply. During our visit the tap water was so loaded with salt-flavored minerals as to be undrinkable. A small pitcher dubbed *rain water* was left in our room refrigerator each day, but the coffee in the breakfast dining room tasted as if it has been made with salty tap water. We were told that four dams have been constructed to catch rain water and that drinking water was actually being imported from the coast. We hope that the rainy season solves this problem and that adequate provision is made for drinking water. We could not help wondering what will happen in dry years when the island's population hits four or five thousand.

Idleness is not a problem at Hamilton, although it is a temptation. The resort boasts the largest fresh water swimming pool in the entire Southern Hemisphere (although this claim is not entirely undisputed), with a central island bar. Activities include tennis ($A6 per hour) on astroturf courts, and a complete gymnasium facility with squash courts, spa, sauna facilities and exercise classes. At the beach there is a full aquatic sports facility with windsurfing, catamaran sailing, parasailing, snorkeling, water-skiing (all with instruction included in the hire cost) fishing dinghy, outrigger canoe, and *war canoe* . All of these activities, except surf skis and outrigger canoes, do have a fee involved. There is also a charge for archery, as well as for the golf flight to neighboring Lindeman Island.

There are several off-island activities offered regularly including access to the Outer Barrier Reef. Hamilton operates *Jet Ranger* helicopters three times a day. These serve the barge the resort has moored at the reef ($A100 per person) allowing two hours for coral viewing, snorkeling, and reef waling. The Hamilton *Quick Cat* departs on Tuesdays at 9:45 a.m. for the 1 1/2 hour trip and three hours on the Reef for swimming, coral viewing, scuba diving (by prior arrangement), reef walking (tides permitting) and a buffet lunch ($A60). There are trips to *Lindeman Island* ($A12), *Dent Island* ($A7), afternoon fishing ($A15), a tour of *Hayman, South Molle* and *Daydream Islands* ($A35), and an all day dive and snorkel trip ($A30). The

Outrigger Resort also offers a one day resort dive course ($A50), with two hours in the pool and an open water dive at a nearby coral reef. No tank refills are available for visiting divers, however.

There is a professionally supervised *Kids Klub* ($A2.50 per hour, $A6 half day, $A12 all day including lunch) between 9:00 a.m. and 5:00 p.m. with games, swimming, contests, crafts, and hikes for the three to twelve year olds. Baby sitting is $A7 per hour, plus $A1 extra per child for other children.

In the spring of 1985, a devastating fire swept through the attractive reception and shops area, destroying the resort's main structure.Undaunted,Keith Williams immediately diverted some of his resident construction crews, started rebuilding and announced fire sale rates for people who wanted to visit the island during the reconstruction. One thing seems certain: Hamilton Island seems here to stay, and is definitely a factor in the future of the Whitsunday Group and of Great Barrier Reef tourism generally.

There are already signs that nearby resorts are becoming increasingly dependent upon Williams' jet airport in preference to the more difficult access through Shute Harbor. Moreover, Williams is spending huge sums – figures up to $200 million are bandied around – in developing Hamilton. Its population will greatly exceed that of any other Barrier Reef resort island, and its facilities and services, including full-time medical staff equipped to do even cosmetic surgery, makes it unique in Northern Queensland. Whether this will become a tacky amusement park, an up-scale haven for discriminating travelers, or something in between remains to be seen.

THE GREAT BARRIER REEF

Outrigger Resort
Hamilton Island
Private Mail Bag, Post Office
Airlie Beach, Queensland 4741
[79] 469 144

Reservations direct to the resort or through Ansett

on Hamilton Island

HASLEWOOD

• no resort • possible pig hunting

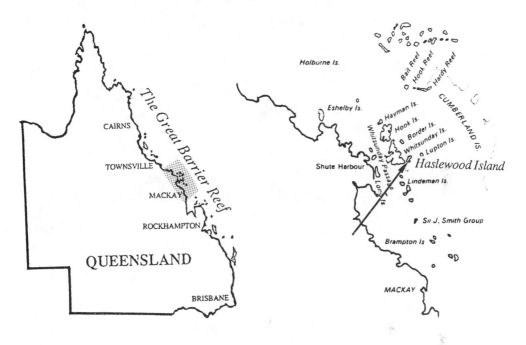

This good-sized island is due east of massive Whitsunday Island. It has no resort. We mention it here because there is reference in local publications to the presence of domestic pigs having been turned loose years ago to run wild on Haslewood for hunting, and you will come across references to this island (also listed are recommendations for times and methods to hunt these animals). Our yacht captain, who seemed very knowledgeable about all of the Whitsunday Passage islands, had never heard of these pigs, however. Although it somehow has acquired a reputation for being a good island to sail to, the currents are difficult and the anchorage not very good.

on Hayman Island

HAYMAN

- coral viewing • national park • bushwalks
- fishing • waterskiing • scuba diving
- anchorage • tennis • golf • sailing
- snorkeling • windsurfing • swimming

THE GREAT BARRIER REEF

Called *the Isle of Smiles,* many people fondly refer to Hayman as the *Honeymoon Island.* Owned by Australia's privately owned Ansett Airlines through its Ansett Hotels subsidiary, this most northerly resort of the Whitsunday group is located about seventeen miles northeast of Shute Harbor and sixty-five miles north of Mackay. Hayman is at the end of the Whitsunday Passage. A national park, all coral and shells are fully protected.

This is probably the best known island of the Whitsunday Group, if not of all Barrier Reef resorts.Early this century, Hayman Island was leased for a sawmill operation. After 1935 it was operated as a fishing resort, and in 1948 Ansett acquired the lease intending to use the island only as the northern destination for its flying boats. Later, Reginald Ansett decided to develop a resort here, and the hotel opened in 1950.The island is of moderate size and is fairly arid, with a low horseshoe-shaped range of hills behind the resort.

The resort side is typical of bush islands.The very pleasant hiking trails are principally on the north side of the island (the back side from the resort) which, because of the way the island faces, is somewhat more rain forest in nature. One of the tracks is a five mile trek around the island, and the shortest is the half mile trek to *Whitsunday Passage Lookout.* Breathtaking southerly views from hilltop, and even from the broad sandy beach in front of the resort, overlook Hook Island and the Whitsunday Passage, and are among the most spectacular among Great Barrier Reef resorts. Around the island you will find wild life and forested ravines, half-mile wide fringing reefs, kookaburras, cockatoos, seagulls, and lori keets. Reputedly, the first tropical palm tree on the island was planted by novelist Zane Grey, and there are now hundreds.

Reached Wednesday, Saturday and Sunday via the *Sea Goddess* (a huge new high speed catamaran ferry) from Hamilton Island, connecting with the Ansett jet flights from Sydney via Brisbane; and on days when there is no Ansett jet service to Hamilton, from Proserpine by Ansett 26 passenger Sikorsky helicopter (20 to 25 minutes, but with a $A145 round trip surcharge). The helicopter also offers charter service which is quite expensive.

There are daily launches from Shute Harbor ($A22 round trip) departing 9:00 a.m. and (on demand) 3:45, returning from Hayman to the mainland at 2:00 p.m. For people needing connection from the airport, a bus operates between Proserpine and Shute Harbor 20 miles daily. Whether you arrive by boat or helicopter, guests are transported from the jetty and heliport, about a half mile from pier to hotel reception area, by Toonerville trolley open-air train.

An alternative way to arrive at Hayman is by Air Whitsunday with three passenger *Lake Buccaneers* from its Whitsunday Field base midway between Airlie Beach and Shute Harbor ($A35 scheduled, $A84 to charter the plane). One lands dramatically in the bay, directly in front of the reception area, and taxis to the beach. You can charter their planes to Hayman from Proserpine ($A150) or Mackay ($A225). Connections are also possible via Air Whit from Townsville ($A96.70), or from Hinchinbrook and Orpheus Islands ($A158).

There are also moorings available for visiting boats ($A5 for day visit and $A20 overnight charge, allowing use of the hotel's facilities), although this is not a favorable anchorage given the fringing reef, the fact that the bay disappears at low tide, and particularly the totally unprotected exposure to both northwest and south winds. A new marina, to be completed shortly, will offer much more secure berthing for smaller boats.

The Royal Hayman Hotel (allowed to be named *Royal* because the Queen was to attend the grand opening, even though circumstances forced her to cancel), consists of blocks of one story and lowrise units. It accommodates 518 guests, to be increased to 600 very shortly. There are five distinct types of accommodations: **Hibiscus** ($A111 per person per night, double occupancy, all meals included), **Frangiapani** and **Palm Lodge** (both $A97), **Poinciana** ($A84), and **North Lodge** ($A70). As with several Whitsunday area resorts, Hayman locally advertises a *stand-by* rate, theirs being $60 for guests who call twenty-four hours before arrival and accept such accommodations as are available at the last minute.

All units have tile showers, telephone, air conditioner, refrigerator, ceiling fans, radio and cable color TV with in-house movies, coffee makers, beach towels, and clothes irons. **Palm Lodges** are in the mid-rise building, have balconies, separate conversation and dressing areas, and a separate swimming pool area restricted for use of guests in these units. The **Hibiscus** units are single-story beachfront rooms, and **Frangipani** occupy the second row away from the beach. Both have verandas and sitting areas.

The massive $A50 million expansion program currently underway will create a huge artificial lagoon incorporating an island pool and bar, add six luxury suites, expand the cabaret to seat more than 400, and refurbish all of the older units.

The main dining rooms are quite large, nicely appointed, and rather unusual among Barrier Reef resorts in that they are very air conditioned. Menus rotate on a weekly basis, and are well planned with good selection. The chef features as main dinner courses roasts (pork, beef, or lamb) or recognizable traditional preparations such as chicken marengo, luau pork or wienerschnitzle, generally offered in very straightforward fashion. The kitchen occasionally forays into the exotic with such choices as Malaysian style beef kebabs, with hot and sour sauce, Kwei Fei, chicken cooked in port wine, or filet de boeuf lacroix (seasoned with chicken liver pate). Fresh fish is available daily. The menu also offers daily (for an extra charge) fresh oysters from the Whitsunday region served natural, Mornay or Kilpatrick. Dinner is served in two seatings, and reservations are a good idea.

The resort claims to have a particularly large wine cellar, although the wine list appeared to us to be very similar to other resorts, priced comparably, and not particularly distinctive. What was very unusual was the fact that house red and white wines are offered in unlimited quantity with meals without charge!

Hayman also has a separate garden restaurant (with indoor and outdoor seating) which they call the *Garden Grill,* when serving breakfast and lunch, and *The Trattoria* when serving dinner. Rather than a buffet lunch, as is served in the main dining rooms, the *Grill* lunch is served at your table and offers a choice of steak, fresh reef fish, shish kebob or sausages (the breakfast type), with self-service salad bar and cheese board. Main course portions were adequate, if small, but the grilled food was very good. The apple pie and fruit salad with ice cream desserts were not at all bad either.

The Trattoria dinner menu is somewhat mind boggling, to say the least – a seven course Italian dinner. You can of course omit any portion you wish, but the food was indeed quite good from start to finish.The meal commences with a choice of soups – either a minestrone or zuppa di pesce alla Genovese (fish soup). Next is the *entrée* (remember, we're in Australia, and this is the introduction course) – both the calamari fritti (fried squid) and spiedino di gamberoni al aglio (grilled prawns with garlic butter) were excellent. Then, of course, the pasta – here try the

on Hayman Island

fettuccine alla marinara, although the spaghetti is also fine. Now, to the main courses: pollo alla fiorentina (chicken braised in a white wine and tomato sauce) was just a little less than anticipated; fettina di manzo alla pizzaiola (steak with tomato herb sauce) was fine; and pesce alla Veneziana (fish sautéed in wine and spices) was excellent. Then, for those who still have room for more, an Italian salad, followed by the cheese board selection, topped off with dessert of the day are included. Try this a least one night.

The hotel also has a poolside *snack bar,* four bars (*Poolside Bar, Whitsunday, Palm Bar,Cabaret Lounge*). *Hernando's Hideaway,* a very noisy all-night beach disco which goes until 4:00 a.m., is thoughtfully situated down the beach, somewhat away from most of the guest rooms. Evening entertainment includes cabaret style floor shows, and the resort features *special nights* – Calypso, South Seas, friendship, Oriental, fancy dress (but not really *fancy* fancy), talent show, etc. The huge cabaret was jammed after dinner, with the older couples and families sitting outside at the lawn furniture on the grass patio looking in, and the boy-meets-girl/girl-meets-boy crowd filling the night club itself. Be aware that Hayman Island does have a certain reputation for attracting the young singles group, and the reputation is not entirely without substance.

As with most Barrier Reef resorts, there is a very pleasant young staff. One thing that struck us about Hayman, however, was the general abundance of staff. People were very friendly and helpful, particularly in the restaurants and the resort seems to have less difficulty keeping its staff complement full than do other resorts in the region.

The bay in front of the **Hayman Island Resort** is virtually completely enclosed by coral reef ,making the lagoon ideal for swimming, skindiving, snorkeling, water skiing, sailing, paraflying and aquaplaning. It is a big bay, but it is definitely full of activity in the afternoons. When the tide is low however, the bay virtually disappears and the muddy bottom is exposed for a good quarter-mile from the beach.

The bay, nearby small islands and sandy bar offer excellent shallow water snorkeling and scuba diving to sixty feet. The bay has a shallow, sloping coral reef, eventually leading out to a vertical wall at forty feet depth, accessible from shore or from Hayman's dive boat. *Dolphin Point*, approached from the dive boat, offers scuba diving from 20-60 feet on rugged terrain from a coral rubble bottom. The resort has full time scuba instructors and offers a one-day *resort course* permitting next-day diving from their boat or, on some days, even from the Outer Reef, accompanied by an instructor. The dive shop was empty when we happened by, and did not appear to be very well stocked with rental gear. We saw nothing for sale there, although it had just been moved to its new location near the helipad, and perhaps will be better stocked later. Tank refills are available for divers with their own equipment.

The **Royal Hayman Resort** aspires to be the *dive capitol* of the Barrier Reef islands. They have arranged to have barges moored at the Outer Reef for day visitors, and regularly run large boat excursions to the reef for snorkeling and diving. In addition, they have just acquired an *Aquascope*, a semi-submersible catamaran with a glass bubble hull. This submarine, built in France, is so maneuverable that it can get to tiny parts of the reef without damaging the coral. It carries eight passengers and allows people who don't dive to appreciate the Outer Reef.

Recent news releases also proclaimed that Ansett is considering installation of a multi-million dollar *Aquaplanet* at the Great Barrier Reef. This is a collection of three to six massive reinforced concrete spheres which float partly submerged. The top, above water, would provide accommodations for sixty hotel guests. The second level, below the water, would be a scuba base as well as providing more hotel or restaurant space. The sub-ocean levels would have windows angled outward at the top for underwater panoramic views. In the center of these floating spheres, Hayman resort envisions one or more floating swimming
pools.

The **Royal Hayman Resort** currently has two tennis courts, with six more under construction. The resort has a weekly tennis tournament, and they are building an international, competition quality center court. The main swimming pool is very attractive, but there sure were a lot of kids in it at one time or another. Other complementary activities include wind surfing, snorkeling, hobi-cat, paddle skis, badminton, ping pong and small catamarans. Everything else is charged for, including the use of deck chairs ($A5 per day or $A25 per week: rental includes beach umbrella and set-up wherever you want), waterskiing ($A4), small motor boats ($A20 per day), glass bottom boat ride ($A2) and paraflying ($A25). There are boat trips to adjacent islands ($A15 each) and as always, weather and tides permitting, to the Outer Reef ($A50). Fishing trips also bring back such catch as coral trout, red emperor, and big game fish like blue fin tuna and black marlin. *Sign-up for all activities is at the main reception desk.*

The resort has a large air conditioned island shop with a broad selection of clothing and other merchandise, including souvenir canvas luggage (in case your collection of tee shirts and other souvenirs now exceeds your original carrying capacity), books, magazines, post cards and sundries. **Hayman** also has a small grocery store, *The Corner Shop* , which sells two-liter *flagons* of red or white wine ($A7.50 each), along with soft drinks, groceries and so forth. You have to ask for the wine which is not on the shelves, but is kept behind the register. There is a bank, hairdresser, medical clinic, post office, and a full Ansett travel office with computer and telephone inter-connection with the airline and other hotels and travel services.

Hayman Island

Ansett's boss, Sir Peter Abel, after looking over the results of the 1984-85 multi-million dollar expansion program, including the 90-room lagoon complex and the new breakwater and yacht moorage, decided that more was needed. In a move, rare among hoteliers, management decreed that **Hayman** would close in July 1985 for nine months until the complete renovation was finished and new undisclosed additions were completed. There seems little doubt that **Hayman** will not succumb to the competition from nearby Hamilton, but instead will maintain a very separate and competitive identity of its own.

Not every reviewer has liked **Hayman.** One even called it *honky-tonk.* It *is* big and bustling. What they could really do without, for example, is the public address system broadcasting throughout the resort, advising individuals that they have a telephone call, that their plane is departing, (which they ought to know anyway) or that paraflying begins in fifteen minutes, whether you are interested or not. It is also unquestionably a professional operation, however, with abundant activities, a diverse clientele, comfortable, if utilitarian, accommodations, and a good kitchen. If you like a busy vacation at a resort similar to those you might expect to find in Hawaii or the more populated Caribbean vacation spots, this could be the best place for you to enjoy the Whitsunday Group and the Great Barrier Reef, particularly with the exciting additions to the resort.

Royal Hayman Island Resort
Hayman Island
via Proserpine, Qld. 4801
[79] 469 100

Reservations through Ansett

turtle returning to the sea – Heron Island

HERON

- coral viewing • national park • bushwalks
- fishing • scuba diving • anchorage • tennis
snorkeling • swimming

THE GREAT BARRIER REEF

This breathtakingly beautiful, small, low island (the highest point of land is just about ten feet above sea level) is a particularly strongly protected national park, about one mile in circumference. Heron is a *true coral cay,* an island made of coral debris and sand, sitting right on the Great Barrier Reef. The only other resort actually part of the Outer Reef is Green Island. Lizard, a continental island, is geographically close to the Outer Reef, but not an integral architectural part of it, and Lady Elliot on the Reef is not a true island resort. Covered by a Pisonia forest, grown to a height of almost 50 feet, and by groves of Pandanus and Casuarina near the beaches, with coconut palms, oaks, coral, sand and grass, both from a distance and up close, Heron Island looks just like the proverbial tropical desert island.

Heron Island is situated in the Capricorn Group, 43 miles northeast of Gladstone. It was first charted in 1843 and was named because of the presence of distinctive white, black and gray herons.Although the home of thousands of birds, the island is perhaps best known as a *breeding ground of giant sea turtles.* One of the island's first commercial enterprises, in fact, was the establishment in 1925 of a turtle soup factory and cannery which also marketed tortoise shell products with little regard for depletion of these venerable and rather scarce animals. In 1932 an attempt was made to establish a resort on the island, but after World War II the effort foundered somewhat. The island became a marine national park in the 1940's, and in 1974 P & O Australia bought an interest in the resort and assumed full control of the resort lease in 1979. They upgraded and refurbished most of the facilities, and established the water desalinization system for the resort.

The waters surrounding Heron Island are a a paradise for scuba, snorkelers and photographers. Manta rays, angelfish, cod – 1150 species of sea life in all swim in these waters. Surrounded by approximately 10 square miles of what well may be the best, most easily accessible coral beds of the entire Barrier Reef region, Heron undoubtedly offers visitors the best reef experience of all Barrier Reef resorts within the least distance from your hotel room. At low tide visitors walk on part of the 15 miles of surrounding Great Barrier Reef without taking a plane or hour-long boat ride with other resorts.

Getting to Heron is itself something of an adventure. The most practical method is via the Helitrans Bell Jet-Ranger 4 passenger or Alouette 6 passenger helicopter from Glastone airport ($A185 round trip). The flight is an exciting thirty to forty minutes, during which the airline provides you with stereo earphones, which eliminate most of the engine noise, through which they play a classical music background accompanied by a commentary from your pilot (they used to have a beautiful recording prepared by the late Richard Burton, but evidently no longer use it) describing the exceptional marine scenery along the way. Flights operate between 9:00 a.m. and 3:00 p.m., connecting with scheduled commercial traffic to Gladstone, according to load and not fixed schedule. There is a fairly strict one suitcase limit if the copters are running full. Air Queensland has several daily flights to Gladstone connecting with TAA and Ansett services to Brisbane or Cairns or Townsville and other major cities.

If you prefer the less expensive approach, or just must carry more gear than the helicopter will handle, there is now an air-conditioned launch service operated by P & O from O'Connell Wharf in Gladstone, departing 8:00 a.m daily except Thursday and Friday ($A90 round trip, 2 1/4 hours). Be aware, however, that this crossing can be *very* choppy. Regrettably for *boaties* , Heron has a poor and very restricted anchorage for yachts, and it's unfortunately a long row ashore, so there isn't much business from charter or private yachts.

Don't count on getting stand-by reservations at **Heron**. It is more often than not fully booked. It has only ninety rooms, accommodating up to 240 guests in motel-type lodges with modern built-ins and reasonably comfortable appointments. Three types of hotel accommodations are available: *lodges* ($A74 per person per day, all meals included) have share facilities and *Reef Suites* ($A112) have private baths. *Heron Suites* ($A131) also have private facilities, a balcony over looking the beach in upstairs units, quarry tiled floors with rugs, higher ceilings and more comfortable cross-ventilation for hot or muggy days. All units have overhead fans, refrigerators, and the ubiquitous tea and coffee making facility. Some rooms have patios. One or two persons may stay in an exclusive *beach house* which the resort offers ($A300). No camping facilities exist on the island, and because of the distance to the coast there is no mechanism for day visits.

One of the first unique things which you will encounter on this naturalists' living museum island is the gooney, but entirely fascinating, migratory *mutton bird,* which regularly returns to the island in late October and leaves exactly five months later. These duck-sized creatures (called *mutton* birds because the flavor of their fatty meat reminded early sailors of the familiar to them taste of mature sheep) are a constant source of interest on the island. They have so much trouble taking off, staggering down the beach almost in a drunken lurch until they gain enough speed to fly, that they are very amusing to watch. Once airborne, they are excellent flyers, and will stay out all day fishing the reef. When they return in the night hours and try to land, however, more often than not they will bump into trees, the ground, or surprised resort guests. They live in nests burrowed under the roots of the tropical trees near the beaches, and their all night meowing noise sounds like a small menagerie of Siamese cats.

The pissonia trees are jammed with *noddy terns,* named because their bobbing heads appear to be mounted on springs. These agreeable birds bring these tropical trees to life. During the resting season we recommend headgear when trekking through the woods. Even if you have never paid much attention to the bird kingdom, it is guaranteed that on Heron Island you will be continually fascinated with the reef herons (after which the island is named), silver gulls, fairy terns, black naped terns, doves, landrails, and the incredible variety of other birdlife.

The spectacle of *giant green turtles,* along with a few loggerheads and hawksbills nesting from late October until April, is one of the most remarkable nature experiences you will ever observe. These giant female turtles drag themselves well up onto the beach, then, through some mysterious instinct, decide on the best place to lay their eggs. After laboriously digging a trench in the sand, they lay several dozen eggs, the size of golf balls, cover them with sand, and then ponderously drag themselves back into the sea and swim away, not to return for perhaps fifty years. They are so intent on what they are about that people can stand quietly and watch this amazing spectacle. Once the eggs have been laid, the turtles are so docile and unafraid that flashbulbs and the close approach of people don't faze them.

Six to ten weeks after the eggs have been so painstakingly

covered, the tiny hatchlings struggle out of the eggs and undertake to defy the almost impossible odds against reaching the sea, contending first with obstacles and birds ashore, crabs at the shoreline, and then hungry denizens of the sea. Few survive, but those that do will return decades later to repeat this breeding cycle. The turtles have been studied and banded for only a couple of decades. Where they go, why they return to this very place, and even exactly how old they are when they produce offspring is still not clearly known.

This is literally an island that is a university. The resort lease covers only one-quarter of the island, with the balance reserved for educational purposes under the auspices of Queensland University. They maintain a substantial facility on the island (a short walk from the resort) and their *Marine Biological Station* displays live specimens of tropical fish and marine life indigenous to the island and its surrounding waters. The staff of the Station is happy to discuss its research with visitors, and a visit to the facility is a must while on the island.

Heron Island hosts a *Skin Divers' Rally* in June and July and *Festival* each November. Quite understandably, this island is a real favorite with scuba divers. The dive shop rents air tanks ($A2 per dive) and some diving gear, including regulators ($A4 per dive), buoyancy compensators ($A4), and wetsuits ($A8). Refills ($A4) are available. Although most Australian tour advisers recommend bringing most of your gear, Heron Island warns you if you intend to take the helicopter that carrying space is limited, and your tanks may come on a later flight when space is available – perhaps days later – and suggests planning to rent tanks on the island. The resort operates two daily snorkel and one-tank guided diving trips to Heron Reef, Wistari Reef, Gorgonian or Rubble Banks, departing 9:15 a.m. and 2:15 p.m.

for 2 hours ($A10 per scuba diver, $A6 per snorkeler). There are 7- and 10-day dive packages (ranging from $A230-300 in addition to the room rates). There is a formal seven day scuba diving instruction program ($A200) commencing on Sundays. This must be booked before arrival, however, and requires a medical certificate and two passport sized photos for enrollment.

There is excellent diving only 250 yards from the boat basin around the *Big Bommie* . The coral bommies 20'to 50' below surface are home to barracuda, kingfish, cod large trout, a variety of tropical fish, delicate fire coral and other beautiful soft corals. Occasionally, outside the fringing reef, one can see humpback whales and killer whales in surrounding waters.

This is an excellent opportunity for some of the world's best underwater photography, particularly since many of the fish have become tame because they have gotten used to hand feeding. Even the shallow waters off the hotel beaches have thousands of beautiful smaller tropical fish of many different types. Just walking around the small island and peering into the shallow waters off the backside of the island, you will most likely see the beautiful, if somewhat shy, rays sporting in the water. Even without the natural life, the soft white sand beaches are an attraction by themselves.

The daily *glass bottom boat* ($A5 per person), carrying up to 25 passengers, takes bags of left-over bread and rolls from breakfast and thereby guarantees that you will see hundreds of tropical fish, including some giant specimens with sharp teeth, so do let go of the roll when the big ones jump out of the water for it, and do not try to hand feed them. In fact, the marine life here in general is particularly accessible to human visitors

THE GREAT BARRIER REEF

because it has become very spoiled. Outside the reef, for example, there lives a shark which has become *too* accustomed to the 11:00 o'clock visit from the *garbo man* , who takes a skiff out with the daily refuse from the resort kitchen. They say that the garbage was late one day, so the shark upended the boat, dumping the startled driver into the water. But the shark wasn't stupid, just hungry, so he let the chagrined garbo man off with just this warning not to be late in the future.

the Barrier Reef near Lizard Island

The resort also offers a 7 1/2 hour reef cruise for up to 30 passengers ($A18 per person), which gives an excellent opportunity for walking on the reef, if the tides are low enough, to inspect the incredible array of animals that live among the coral. This activity is particularly tide and weather sensitive, however, so if reef walking is a principle reason for your visit, be sure to check local tide tables, or telephone the resort for tide information, to see if the tides will coincide with the dates of your visit.

The staff conducts an outstanding two hour *walking tour* of the island each morning, pointing out and explaining the incredible array of natural life all over the island. Do take this easy walk, but remember to wear a hat! Each year two weeks are set aside especially for the serious naturalist. *Bird Week* in December of each year, and *Reef Week* in February of each year.These involve lectures, discussions, projects and field excursions which are led by a team of expert lecturers in the fields of ornithology, marine biology and photography. Advance registration is essential to participate in these events.

Heron is a reasonably complete resort with other things to do beside enjoying the surroundings, if you have time or energy for other activities after spending hours in the almost hypnotically beautiful waters. There are tennis courts, which are more often than not in terrible shape, so not for the serious player. A friend of ours calls this *hit and giggle* tennis. A couple of times a week there are day cruises to nearby islands for a day on the beach, snorkeling from the beach of a different island, and a popular barbecue luncheon. Fishing trips to waters, outside the limits of Heron Island National Park, are available aboard the 35' M.V. Christine ($A15 per person for half day, $A25 full day, gear included) where you may catch groper, kingfish, mackerel, red emperor, coral trout, coral cod and sweetlip.

The resort does not have the usual collection of catamarans, windsurfers, water tricycles, and small motorboats that you find at most other resorts. However, there is the swimming pool, volley ball, ping pong, and the usual selection of island resort entertainments.

Dining was not the strongest reason for visiting Heron Island. We were possibly tougher on Heron than with other resorts,because owned as they are by an elegant passenger steamship line, we were led to expect cuisine of particular distinction. Food is definitely abundant and hearty, although perhaps just a bit too contrived. There is a choice of three main courses each evening, but why the chef feels the urge to try to prepare veal Cordon Bleu for two hundred people simultaneously, we cannot fathom.The barbecue steaks and chops are so superior. Unfortunately, again for reasons not clear to us, the fresh fish seemed bland, and not as enjoyable as from several other Barrier Reef resort kitchens. We should hasten to point out that dinner is a very social time in the dining commons, and most people sit at the larger tables and become acquainted with their fellow visitors. If you enjoy a hearty and pleasant evening meal, this is indeed a fun time to share the day's superb adventures.

Evening activities in the resort center around the well stocked *Turtle Bar* or the *Pandanus Lounge* disco. There are movies most nights, and there is a live band for dancing two nights a week. The resort is large enough that you will have little difficulty making new acquaintances and sharing experiences over a relaxing drink. The real nightlife, however, is the natural life, with *nighttime strolls* along the beach, particularly during the summer (December - February), to see the mutton birds and the turtles, to count the myriad stars, to listen to the surf.

Perhaps you have guessed that we very much like Heron Island. To many people, Heron Island is one of the world's truly special places. It is not that the resort is especially luxurious ,but rather the island itself, which brings the spectacle of nature to you with less effort and in more comfort than anywhere else in the entire world.

Heron Island
via Gladstone, Qld. 4680

[79] 781 488

Reservations through P & O Resorts, 14252 Culver Drive, Suite A-316, Irvine, California 92714; telephone [714] 786-0119 or [800] 472-5015

aerial view of Hinchinbrook

HINCHINBROOK

• coral viewing • national park
• bushwalks • fishing • waterskiing
• anchorage • snorkeling • swimming

THE GREAT BARRIER REEF

This tremendous island is the world's largest island national park. It is more than ten times the size of Manhattan Island, and one of the largest islands in the southern hemisphere. Alan Lucas, author of *Cruising the Coral Coast* , described Zoe Bay at the southeast end of Hinchinbrook as

> *perhaps the most beautiful place on the entire east coast of Australia. The beach is gently sloping, hard sand backed by low native scrub interspersed with tropical foliage and palms. In the background, soaring skyward, are the spectacular mountains of Hinchinbrook's backbone.*

From the north end of the island where the resort is situated, there are stunning views of Goold and Brooks Islands.

With Dunk Island, Hinchinbrook shares the distinction of being one of Australia's two coastal *tropical* islands resorts. The other resorts to the south, until you reach Heron, are situated on *bush* islands. Located approximately one hundred miles south of Cairns, and an equal distance north of Townsville, it is about fifteen miles off the coast from Cardwell. Because of its massive size, Hinchinbrook, from a distance, appears to be part of the mainland. It is separated from the mainland, however, by the Hinchinbrook Channel, a long underwater fault valley.

The western edge of Hinchinbrook is characterized by tropical green vegetation with mountains behind. On the eastern side, you are overwhelmed with the beauty of palm fringed bays with wide sandy beaches set between rocky headlands. The island is covered with tropical vegetation. It has dense rain forests (one of which is the densest in Australia), six picturesque mountains over 3000 feet tall, abundant wildlife and plunging waterfalls, and mangrove waterways (including one with a plank bridge where scientists are studying the ecology of such groves).The mangrove tree is special because, although it grows at the edge of bodies of salt water, it is a fresh water tree. The secret is in its complex root and leaf system making it a natural desalinization plant – one which man has only recently finally been able to copy in a rudimentary fashion after years of study and experimentation.

Hinchinbrook Island is also the highest on the Queensland coast – 3650 feet at *Mount Bowen,* and the western half is where Australia's highest rainfall is recorded. The island has no permanent inhabitants other than the resort operators. Remnants of stone fish-traps and cave paintings indicate that Aboriginals lived there at least seasonally. The decision has been made by Australian authorities and the resort operators to preserve this national natural treasure, so very little additional development will take place, even in conjunction with the resort property.

Hinchinbrook is somewhat difficult to reach. The resort has no airfield and no intention of building one. From Townsville, there is a 13-passenger seaplane service landing near the resort jetty on Wednesdays, Saturdays and Sundays aboard Air Whitsunday ($A68.50 each way). Interestingly, Hinchinbrook is thus coincidentally one of the very few barrier reef resorts with a direct air connection to another resort island. This is solely because the seaplane service out of Townsville makes an intermediate stop at Orpheus Island on the way to or from Hinchinbrook, if there is a reserved passenger, although neither resort advertises this link. Air Whitsunday service also connects with that from the Whitsunday Group, so you can string together flights to Hinchinbrook from Airlie Beach or Hayman Island ($A158) or Hamilton Island ($A193).

If you are not approaching Hinchinbrook by air from

THE GREAT BARRIER REEF

Townsville (or Orpheus), the problem is getting to Cardwell conveniently. Once there, opposite the island and roughly fifteen miles away, launches depart for the island at 9:00 a.m. (considering the small distance, a somewhat costly $A20 per person, $A80 to charter) for the short ride daily, except Monday. Monday is the *quiet* day on this quietest of islands, with no scheduled arrivals or departures or formal activity.

Occasionally boats from nearby Orpheus Island to the south include Hinchinbrook on their itinerary. There are also fairly regular boat cruises operating from Cardwell to the northern (resort) section of the island, and coastal cruise service from Cardwell to Lucinda through the spectacular channel. You can also hire a bareboat or houseboat at Cardwell. The usually calm waters of the Hinchinbrook Channel provide safe boating even for inexperienced sailors, and the charter operators provide necessary basic training prior to departure.

If you have any difficulty planning your transportation to or from Hinchinbrook, however, fear not, for the resort staff is incredibly understanding and helpful in seeing to it that guests arrive and depart as conveniently and inexpensively as possible. Should you be sailing (motor or sail), Hinchinbrook invites *boaties* and offers excellent anchorage as well as fuel (if you order ahead).

The resort at Cape Richards is set above Orchid Bay, a beautiful bay beach by anyone's standards, situated on the northernmost tip of the island. When you step from your boat, plane or launch, you will be warmly greeted by the island's most genial and helpful young proprietors, Peter and Jan Phillips. They are shareholders in the small group which owns the resort operation, but recently have taken on the entire management responsibility from the management concern which the owners previously engaged. We have rarely encountered two people more dedicated to helping their guests have a superb time and enjoy the beauties of their island. Although their staff changes fairly regularly, as with many of the small island resorts, the Phillips seem to have a knack for attracting exceptionally pleasant and friendly employees.

While Peter and Jan invite you into the restaurant/bar/commons next to the fresh water swimming pool for a cool refreshment on arrival, the truck (if that is what you call one of the oldest living flat beds in the world) will transport your luggage to one of fifteen two room bungalows. The bungalows are large, self-contained units, all with filtered sea views through the trees, with double and two single beds with divider curtain (to split the room in two if you wish, for example if you have children in the same room) in one room, bath room in the center, and lounge and living room area with a large refrigerator, a kitchen sink, counter, table and day bed in the other room. ($A85-95 per person per day, double occupancy, with all meals; children 3 to 15 charged $A22 only for meals.) The rooms are very simple and very rustic.

After meeting your hosts and the resort staff and inspecting your accommodations, you will be offered the chance to have another drink, try the beaches, take a walk through the forest, use their water sport facilities or just be lazy. Whatever you decide, the staff will display an uncommon and continuing friendly interest in helping you enjoying yourselves to the maximum.

Having undoubtedly taken a prompt liking to this friendly place, you will be pleased to discover that the meals are simple, yet simply excellent. The chef hired in November 1984 has real talent. His only vice is that he has an Australian army cooking back ground, and seems to feel that the volume of food must be large enough at each meal to fortify you for the Battle of the Bulge. For such a tiny facility the resort also boasts a quite fine Australian wine list and well stocked bar.

Morning and noon meals are served in or outside the dining room, although they will gladly prepare a small continental breakfast for the following morning which you may take back to your room after dinner, and they almost force generous picnic lunches on you if you have the slightest desire to explore other parts of this huge national park. Don't miss their served lunch, however. The choice of cold chicken or fresh reef fish, lightly breaded, or a generous rump steak might tempt you to eat three lunches. Like everything else here, dress is super casual.

Around the dining area, you will almost certainly have one or two or three of the friendly wallabies (often with a *joey*, or *baby,* which continues to live in her pouch until perhaps six months of age) politely inquiring if you have any extra scraps of bread or melon rind for her. The older wallabies, particularly the males, become quite territorial and leave the commons area. The younger ones, however, delight in visiting the tourists.

In addition to these small marsupials, you will see a few *goanas* (what we call iguanas), also known as monitor lizards, perhaps two or three feet in length. They are quite shy and will give you a wide berth. Locals will advise you that when alarmed the monitor lizard makes for the nearest tree on the run and will climb out of danger. If you encounter one out in the bush where, unlike Hinchinbrook, there are no nearby trees, old timers tell you that you must flap your arms and wave your hands so these poor lizards will not try to climb on you with their rather sharp claws.

The beach, just down the hill from the restaurant area, is one of the most beautiful in Great Barrier Reef country and indeed one has to look carefully even in the United States to find such beaches. The sand runs well into the ocean, unlike the mud flats that are exposed around other Barrier Reef islands at low tide, and there is reasonably good snorkeling around the rocks at the end of the beach.

Remember, though, that this is a national park and natural life is left entirely alone, including the sand flies and other insects. It is well worth the small investment to stop in the shop behind the bar and pick up a bottle of Rid or some other effective insect repellent cream as soon as you check in, and use it promptly and generously during your stay on Hinchinbrook.

There are laundry facilities available. Phone calls must be made or received in the office. There is a small souvenir and sundries shop next to the office. There is no disco, no band, no movies, no TV, no room radios, no intrusion into your enjoyment of the national park.

The resort has no organized activities and doesn't need any. This is one of the world's great relaxation and nature paradises. The resort provides paddle surfboards, windsurf equipment, and a canoe. You can fish from the rocks or their pontoon. For a small charge, they will take you by boat over to the nearby Brooks Islands for outstanding snorkeling within the protected fringing reef, and lazying on an outstanding beach. For sheer abundance of fish and variety of underwater life, the small ecosystem around Brook rivaled that seen anywhere in northeast

THE GREAT BARRIER REEF

Australia! The water is relatively shallow (less than ten feet in the fringe reef area) and quite calm. This is excellent snorkeling country by any standard.

The staff will direct you to the best paths for bush walking, where you can sit in the forest and observe some of the three hundred different species of birds that inhabit the island. If you

on Hinchinbrook Island

are lucky you will see the blue Ulysses butterflies and at Mangrove Bay (which Peter Phillips calls *Turtle Bay*), some giant turtles. With a permit, camping is allowed at Macushla Point on the west side of the island.

For years **Hinchinbrook Resort's** motto has been that the maximum population of the island is thirty people (although they may be forgiven for not including children of guests in this census, thereby allowing a massive population explosion to fifty or so when the island is fully booked). We understand, however, that a people boom may be in the works – to *sixty* guests– by remodelling some of the bungalows.This   correspondingly would probably reduce the number of children visitors, and the relative impact on this 231 square mile island would be perhaps one additional person per twenty-five wallabies.

If you have ever visited, or thought you would enjoy visiting, a national park or just need to commune with nature for a few days to recharge your overworked mental batteries, Hinchinbrook Island will provide a fantastic holiday for you. As they say on their stationery, this friendly resort is *a million miles from the nearest disco*. Such uncrowded and unspoiled natural splendor is too rare.

Hinchinbrook Island Resort
P.O. Box 3
Cardwell, Qld. 4816

Reservations direct to the resort or through Ansett.

Hook Island

HOOK

- unoccupied • observatory • scuba diving
- snorkeling • camping

THE GREAT BARRIER REEF

This is one of the world's most beautiful, essentially unoccupied islands, being undeveloped except for the observatory and adjacent facilities on its eastern point. Located opposite Hayman Island to the northwest, and almost touching the point of Whitsunday Island to the east, this second largest island in the Whitsunday Group has many of the more important scuba dive and snorkel sites in the region. The *Pinnacle* has excellent corals. The *Woodpile* has a near vertical wall that drops to 110 feet, and is definitely not for snorkelers. *Manta Ray Bay* has gullies and tunnels. At the northern end of the island is *Butterfly Bay*, where you will find what in our estimation is some of the finest and easiest snorkeling available anywhere for viewing abundant coral and thousands of fish. In addition, if you go ashore, you may see large colonies of *blue tiger butterflies*, with black wings covered with pale blue spots. Look for them in shaded valleys with dense vegetation.

The air-conditioned *observatory* with forty viewing windows ($A5 admission and not really that exciting if you are a snorkeler) is situated on a point off Hook Island on a narrow channel separating Hook from Whitsunday Island. It is now owned by the Telford Hotel group, which owns and operates the South Molle Island Resort, and brings guests to the observatory regularly from the resort for sightseeing, glass bottom boat trips, or overnight camping. Their boats, however, serve only the jetty at the observatory. To reach the important dive and snorkeling sites, special arrangements must be made to charter a boat or arrange transport by one of the launches from Shute Harbor. The observatory is also reached from Shute Harbor by a day trip via the Telford catamaran ($A20) or the Hamilton Quick Cat ($A30).

Camping is permitted near the observatory ($A3 per person per day). There is also camping at the south end of the island, operated by a company which sells, at substantial prices, week long camping vacations with transportation to the island. Tents, food, and some daily water activities are included. Some local residents, while having no objection to individual groups of campers, resent the commercial use of this national park island by these entrepreneurs. There are no tourist accommodations per se on the island other than the showers, toilets, well, beer garden, gift shop and coffee shop maintained by Telford at the observatory.

If you are sailing in the Whitsundays, Hook Island offers the two finest sheltered anchorages in the Whitsunday Passage – *Nara* and *Macono* – on its south coast. These two long narrow inlets are surrounded by hills and resemble fjords. They are placid and beautiful and often the over-night location for charter boats, particularly when weather threatens.

on Hook Island

Lizard Island

LADY ELLIOT

- coral viewing • national park • bushwalks
- fishing • scuba diving • anchorage • tennis
- snorkeling • swimming • camping

THE GREAT BARRIER REEF

Forty miles south of Heron Island and 190 miles north of Brisbane, Lady Elliot is at the southern-most point of the Great Barrier Reef and is located on the Outer Reef itself. Part of the Bunker Group Islands, it is a *true coral cay* and is surrounded by coral reefs. In 1886 a kerosene pressure lighthouse was established on the island. It is still available for inspection, and is an excellent diving spot, where you can see schools of 15 foot manta rays. There is even an old paddle steamer for wreck-diving. Scuba instruction is available for beginners. In addition to excellent snorkeling opportunities, the island has a glass bottom boat for coral and fish observation.

Access is by air from Brisbane via 1 3/4 hour flight on Barrier Reef Airways ($A198.50 round trip) or 30 minutes from Bundaberg or Maryborough ($A90 round trip). Flights are also available from the Gold Coast south of Brisbane, the Sunshine Coast north of Brisbane, and nearby Herbey Bay. Due to weight restrictions, personal luggage is usually restricted to one suitcase (22 pounds) per person; sleeping bags and pillows can be carried separately. Day trips ($A95) from Bundaberg or Maryborough include round trip air fare, conducted reef walks (subject to tides and winds), a glass bottom boat ride and lunch. For sailors, the anchorage is particularly difficult and not recommended for amateurs.

Lady Elliot has virtually no development at all. Accommodations for up to 50 people are in new beachfront cabins ($A55 per person per day, meals included) and 12x12 safari tents ($A45), with raised timber floors covered in seagrass matting, with bunk and double beds with foam mattresses. The resort has bush-type showers and three flush toilets. Meals are served in the central dining area, and there are tropical barbecues on the beach. The staff will prepare picnic lunches for you. There is an island bar. Rates include use of snorkel equipment, a conducted reef walk (subject to tides and weather), one ride in a glass bottom boat or fishing trip.

On this island you enjoy the sea, watch the turtles and the frigate birds, snorkel to your heart's content and perhaps learn to scuba dive. The resort operation here is new. If all this sounds good, and if you want to have the distinction of having been to the very southern end of the Great Barrier Reef, and if you happen to be visiting the Gold Coast or Sunshine Coast (other very popular resort areas of Australia's east coast), this island could have strong appeal for you.

Lady Elliot Island Resort
c/o Barrier Reef Airways
General Aviation Area
Brisbane Airport, Qld. 4007
[7] 268 6255

Reservations through Barrier Reef Airways or through SO/PAC, 1448 15th Street, Suite 105, Santa Monica, California 90404; telephone [213] 393 8262

on Dunk Island

on Lizard Island

LADY MUSGRAVE

• no resort • day trips • coral cay
• atoll lagoon • snorkeling

This unusual coral cay, south of Fairfax Island and north of Lady Elliot Island in the Bunker Group, has a perfect atoll lagoon with a deep narrow entrance ,probably dug or blasted by Japanese fishermen early this century. It is about 30 miles from the coast and possesses a beautiful long circular reef, which sweeps away from the islet to the south and loops back to the north to the single deep entrance. *It is without accommodations* and historically was visited by serious sailors. A stop here is included on Air Whitsunday's 5-day Flying Boat Adventure from Cairns to Brisbane. Barrier Reef Sea Adventures has just added a day trip aboard the catamaran *MV Lady Musgrave,* departing 7:30 a.m. from Bundaberg for $A60, including lunch, which allows swimming in the lagoon, snorkeling in the coral garden, a glass bottomed boat trip, island and reef walks with experienced guides. Scuba diving can also be arranged through them.

on Lindeman Island

LINDEMAN

- coral viewing • national park • bushwalks
- fishing • waterskiing • anchorage • tennis • golf
- sailing • snorkeling • windsurfing • swimming

THE GREAT BARRIER REEF

This is the most southerly and oldest (established 1929) of the resorts grouped fairly closely in the Whitsunday Islands, and is near the southern entrance to the Whitsunday Passage. Lindeman is 40 miles northeast of Mackay. The leasehold to the island was purchased in 1905 by Captain James Adderton, a coastal explorer, who stocked it with sheep. In 1923 a subsequent purchaser converted it for tourist development, and in 1974 P & O Australia (which also operates Heron Island, the coral cay resort in the Capricorn group) bought the major interest in the leasehold and took over operation of the resort.

Called the *Family Island,* it is one of the largest resort islands (but not largest resorts) in the Whitsunday Group, although considerably smaller than the unoccupied islands of the area – Whitsunday, Hook, and even nearby Shaw, just to the south. The terrain provides protection from the prevailing winds. Some of the island's beaches are much less rocky than others in the region, and the views from the hilltops are superb. Lindeman is also fortunate in having readily available fresh water. There are scattered bushlands and there is ample bird life. Blue tiger butterflies with blue spotted black wings are found in abundance in Butterfly Valley.

Lindeman is reached most directly by light aircraft daily from Mackay via Lindeman Aereal Service, 20 to 25 minutes on twin engine Aztec/Shrike Commander or Britten Norman Islander ($A45 each way) by 25 minute flight from Proserpine daily ($A40 each way) or from Hamilton Island ($A22.50 each way). There are also frequent launches from Shute Harbor. Day visits to Lindeman depart from Mackay, Shute Harbor ($A30 via the Hamilton Quick Cat), Proserpine and nearby Whitsunday area islands. Hamilton Island Resort also flies guests over directly to play golf. There is a fairly good yacht anchorage at the resort, although if the winds are unpredictable it is probably better to anchor either in the bay at the southeast end of the island sheltered by Shaw Island, or in Boat Port on the north side facing Pentecost Island depending upon from which direction the prevailing winds are blowing.

Lindeman Island Resort prides itself on its easy going lifestyle. It boasts clean ,simple accommodations with 92 private rooms for up to 362 guests. There is a standby rate ($A49) for guests willing to calling one day ahead and willing to accept space available. The resort offers many discount and promotion packages. For example, every family stay of three nights or more includes one child's accommodation and free meals. All apartments have private bath, shower, double beds, seating area, ceiling fans, refrigerator, coffee maker. Laundry facilities are available in each building for the use of all guests.

The resort has three different types of accommodations. **Whitsunday Units** ($A85 per person per day, meals included) accommodate up to six and are situated on the beach front or in elevated blocks with views of Kennedy Sound. These are the most expensive and nicely appointed rooms. Most have excellent views to the south. **Uphill units** are served by a delightful old fashioned four passenger *inclinator* –a cog wheel transport which takes you up the hillside. **Leilani Units** ($A78) overlook the beach. **Tradewinds Units** ($A65) overlook the resort's pool and gardens, and are lower in price because the view is not quite as pleasant and the rooms are subject to more noise from the pool area. **Leilani** and **Tradewinds** units sleep four.

The hotel has a single large dining room with adequate food. *The Chart Room,* still listed in many travel publications and supposed to feature a separate a la carte menu, closed some two years year ago, and based upon our experience in the dining room, more's the pity. The resort has two cocktail lounges, one adjacent to the dining room in the central complex, and the other next to the pool in the same tiny building used by the dispensary from 3:00 - 3:30. There is a disco a few nights a week, cabaret nights, dancing in the bar most evenings, and live music or entertainment every night. The resort has pool tables, movies, bingo, and *indoor horse-racing* .

The particularly well stocked island shop bills itself as a *profit-free shop and a good place to buy watches, cameras, radios and tape-recorders*. Actually, it seems just a very pleasant, somewhat above average resort store with a very nice staff. There is also a bank agency, as well as a snack bar at the resort.

There are eight beaches for guests at Lindeman, as well as access to nearby *Seaforth* and *Shaw Islands*. You can play tennis on a court lighted for night play. You can also golf on a very distinctive 6-hole course split by the light aircraft runway but with exceptional views; Hamilton Island flies its golfing guests to Lindeman to enjoy this course. The resort also offers water skiing, gaffer sailing, sailing instruction, snorkeling (but clearly not the best in the region), fishing, surf ski, water polo and water volley ball, flight seeing, free cruises, catamaran sailing, a small, but very attractive swimming pool, in a lush tropical setting, cricket, softball, and cruises to other islands.

The island is a national park with twelve miles of scenic nature trails and bush walking. Near the resort one finds scores of rainbow lorikeets (multicolored parrots).You can take a pleasant walk to the dam which supplies water for the golf course and the resort. In the area there are ducks, swamp hens, cormorants, sulphur crested cockatoos and more lorikeets. Kayaks are available for use at the dam.

The resort makes a special point of catering to families. They offer free group play activities for children three to eight every morning. Children's activities include hikes, barbecues, races, sand castle building, treasure hunts, ping pong. The resort staff will care for your children for you while you dine in the evening. For children over eight, there is a special island summer camp, *Adventure Valley,* where children live-out pioneer style in a camp settlement for up to three days with qualified adult *Adventure Leaders.*

Lindeman is busy, pleasant, and criss-crossed with beautiful walks offering excellent vistas of almost the entire southern Whitsundays. It is, in our opinion, not the best of resorts or the worst of resorts, but it has its loyal following and is often fully booked.

Lindeman Island
Lindeman Island, Qld. 4741
[79] 469 333

Reservations through P & O Resorts, 14252 Culver Drive, Suite A-316, Irvine, California 92714; telephone [714] 786-0119 or [800] 474-5015

Lizard Island

LIZARD

- coral viewing • national park
- fishing • waterskiing • scuba diving
- anchorage • tennis • golf • snorkeling
- windsurfing • swimming • bushwalks

THE GREAT BARRIER REEF

Visited by princes and prime ministers, movie stars and magnates, Americans and Europeans, this is a large (2500 acres) granite island with magnificent, beautiful fringing coral. There are not enough superlatives to describe the island's *Blue Lagoon* on its south coast. For natural beauty and professionalism of operation, this is a world- class resort.

This resort is by far the most northerly of the Barrier Reef vacation islands, located well within the tropics at only 14° 40' latitude south of the equator, sixty miles or so northeast of Cooktown, and 145 miles north of Cairns, well up the Cape York peninsula. Lizard is a granite island close to the Outer Barrier Reef. Because of the way the reef is segmented and broken up, the resort advertises that it is actually a part of the Great Barrier Reef itself although, unlike the coral cays Green, Heron and Lady Elliot to the south, this is not structurally or architecturally precisely so.

The island was named by Captain Cook during charting of the Barrier Reef in 1770, when he noted several monitor lizards (iguanas) over three feet long. This is a high continental island somewhat barren in patches, with mountains, a few stands of rain forest, some examples of mangrove swamp and other tropical vegetation, and dozens of birds of the region, but no indigenous wild game.

Originally this was an aboriginal ceremonial ground. Only adult males visited the island during certain seasons for their religious purposes. The sad story of Captain Watson and his wife, Mary Phillips Watson, is preserved in her diary and other records on display in the museum at Cooktown. In 1880 he was in the *beche de mere* or sea cucumber trade, a commodity prized particularly in the orient at the time. He left his wife, young son and Chinese servants to go off with his crew to pursue his trade on islands to the north. The natives found the presence of a woman and an uninitiated young man a terrible sacrilege, and when Captain Watson and his men were unexpectedly detained, natives of the area attacked. One of the servants was killed immediately and carried off. Mrs. Watson, her son, and remaining wounded servant set themselves afloat in a large tub used for boiling the *beche de mere*, only to die of dehydration just before a tropical storm would have provided them with drinking water. Captain Watson returned to find his family destroyed and later, as it is told, died of a broken heart. Remnants of the walls of the Watson house still stand as a reminder of this early attempt to settle the island.

The island has abundant fresh water. Paw paw (papaya) trees, poinsettias, and other tropical flowers and palms grow abundantly. Because this is a national park island, the government regulates strictly what vegetation may be imported, even for landscaping the resort, so the facility makes ample use of the many varieties of plants and flowers which exist indigenously.

What makes this a particularly desirable island is that it is surrounded by a superb example of fringing coral reef with some of the best coral on the entire Barrier Reef. There are miles of beaches and twenty-four sandy coves. The water around this island is clear; at times startlingly clear. You can see the coral and fish from out of the water, and fishermen sometimes stalk their prey by sight here.

Lizard is most easily reached by a fifty minute Air Queensland flight from Cairns ($A203.80 round trip) daily except Thursday. The flight to Lizard, taking you over dozens and dozens of awesome patches of the Great Barrier Reef, itself is the type of sightseeing trip that other resorts offer as a costly extra. There are no day boat trips to Lizard; it is simply too removed from the mainland. Air Queensland, during part of the year, does operate day flights out of Cairns (approximately $A150 including flight and barbecue lunch) to permit a brief visit to the island. The *goonies* (so named because they so often come to marvel at the Blue Lagoon) are provided with their own special hut with changing rooms and lounge area. Because of the fringing reef, the island has a superb yacht anchorage.

At the airport you are met by the staff and driven to the central lodge. First comes a complimentary welcome cocktail and first-name introductions all around. This informality is characteristic of the resort, so that staff members even addressed Australia's Prime Minister and his wife by their first names during their visit. The exceptionally personable staff has been well recruited from all over Queensland, and been carefully instructed to make all guests feel at home.

After your relaxing introduction, you are taken to your bungalow where your luggage already awaits you. As you walk to your room, you will immediately be impressed by the beautiful landscaping with large expanses of tailored lawn so difficult to maintain in the sandy soil and tropical heat, and a variety of flowers around each building. All of this leads down to a lovely white sand beach and the sheltered bay.

Lizard Island Lodge ($A150 per person per day, all meals included, except during September-November for Marlin season; then $A165; a few slightly larger *executive* units at $A180 and $A210; stand-by rates,$A105, three night maximum, for bookings within 48 hours of arrival) was formerly closed January-March, and is now open all year around.The entire resort is modeled throughout after an Australian pioneer homestead with a large veranda. The roofs on all the buildings slope upwards from the front to the back of the bungalows, providing good ventilation and, with the overhead fans, draining the tropical heat quite nicely.

The recently expanded operation has accommodations for only sixty people, and they firmly say that will be the absolute maximum. The comfortably appointed bungalow units- (two per single story building) – overlooking Anchor Bay and have patios facing beachfront, king and single bed, carpeting, refrigerators (restocked daily with wine, beer, spirits, chocolates, and Lizard Island fruit cake). On arrival, the staff has provided a small plate of fresh fruit in each room. Each room has the ubiquitous tea/coffee maker, as well as an iron and ironing board, a beach umbrella and rain umbrella, and beach mats for two. There are no radios, televisions or telephones. Baths are simple and adequate. Unfortunately, in a very few of the units the bathrooms abut, and act as excellent sound conductors to the next bungalow.

The redecorated and carpeted common area, including the elegant dining complex, is in soft whites and pastels. An entire wall of windows allows beautiful views of the resort and the bay. To one side of the reception area is the small store with a limited selection of resort wear, sundries and souvenirs.There is an attractive intimate bar for before dinner cocktails and complementary hot hors d'oeuvres each evening. In the dining room, tables for each meal are set with elegant formal service, and even foods put out on the small buffet are decorated with taste and an appreciation for appearance. Excellent quality, very attractive meals feature an emphasis on salads, freshly caught reef fish, fresh fruits. The restaurant has, in fact, won an award as one of Australia's best resort kitchens.

Breakfasts start with a buffet selection of fruit juices, fresh fruits and cold cereals. Hot breakfasts of eggs, done any way you wish, omelets, fresh fish, steaks, other meats, pancakes, or almost anything else you might ask for, are readily available. Served lunches offer a choice of fish or meat, always excellent, and you may opt to be served out on the veranda overlooking the bay.

Dinners always begin with an excellent imaginative entrée. One night a choice between stilton and onion soup or avocado and scallops, another evening between pumpkin and apple soup or grilled Moreton Bay bugs, or perhaps minestrone soup or smoked salmon and avocado in filo pastry.

Main courses for dinner always present at least three selections, one of which will be fresh fish and the other an excellent steak. Some nights the third choice might be fine lamb, roast pork or veal. One night a week there is a seafood buffet, which can only be described as picturesque. There is a fine selection of wines at middling to higher resort prices ($A12 and up), with a perfectly drinkable inexpensive carafe wine always available ($A6.50). Fresh coffee at all meals is served in individual French *filtre* pots for each table.

One thing which we appreciated was the fact that you could elect to make meals a very sociable time or, if you felt private and romantic, ask for a table for two. Most often, however, people were so friendly that groups of four and six would form over cocktails and adjourn to the dining room to get better acquainted over dinner. Though cordial and charming, service by this well trained staff was at all times impeccable and thoughtful.

Lizard Island is an international Game Fishing Association weighing station and base for marlin boats during the game fishing season. It boasts some of the world's *outstanding game fishing waters* outside of the excellent fringing coral reef. During the September-November season, black marlin, often over 1000 lbs., are taken. Except for record-breakers, most are tagged and released.

The resort virtually guarantees that you will hook plenty of fish here. The sailing boat, with its experienced crew, almost assures non-stop catches. There are abundant large sailfish, blue fin tuna, bonita, mahi mahi, barracuda, spanish mackeral, red emperor, grey snapper, and coral trout among dozen of the other varieties, and the pleasure fishing is excellent year-round. The chef is delighted to cook your catch, and many guests share their good fortune with other guests of the resort in the form of *sashimi* or other appetizers or hot lunches. Some Australian guests had their large catch cut into fillets, frozen and packed into coolers, which the management permitted them to use to take their prize from resort to home freezer, when they departed!

The island features good scuba diving within thirty minutes of the resort, as well as various spots along the Great Barrier Reef with such picturesque names as *Cook's Passage, Dynamite Passage, Shrimp Caves* and *Big Bommie.* In the *Cod Hole,* you can see and pet the giant potato cod which lives there in thirty foot reef-protected waters. The island offers diving instructions and sends guides along on dive trips. There is a dive package ($A50 per person per day) which includes two tank dives, air, weight belt, dive boat and guide. You can rent regulators, gauges, and BCs. Wetsuits or photographic gear are not available.

Lizard Island offers some of the best skin diving in the Coral Sea and South Pacific (or even elsewhere in our experience). You can walk right into Anchor Bay towards Prince Charles Island, at the left edge of the resort's beach, and see angel fish of all colors, butterfly fish, parrot fish, trout, snapper, and even an occasional crustacean. The size of these tropical fish is most exciting compared to other island snorkeling. There are also very impressive coral formations with a lot of blue tip staghorn, and Watson's Bay, adjacent to the Lodge is the home of some of the largest giant clams, with huge colorful mantels, you will see anywhere. The resort thoughtfully gives you a map with the best snorkeling areas around the island and its neighbors plainly and accurately marked.

Climb *Cook's Look* ! This is the ridge running across the island adjacent to Watson Bay and was the peak from which Captain Cook examined the reef for evidence of a passage. The view from the top of this 1167' palisade is absolutely breathtaking. You can see the whole island, the *Blue Lagoon,* the bays, outer islands, the whole Lizard reef structure, and the mainland in the distance. It will take the hardy climbers about forty-five minutes, and the more relaxed vacationer perhaps two hours in each direction. There is some clambering up granite slabs, so take good ripple-sole or deck shoes for traction. Stop at the reception desk for a canteen full of fresh water before you start out, for the climb can be dehydrating.

At the summit, you will find a commemorative stone marker and a brass plaque indicating the distances to various points in the world. Be sure to sign the book stored in the plastic box under the monument at the top, and don't forget to sign in *again* at the reception desk after your climb. (The staff doesn't climb the peak each day to see who has been there.) For your efforts, you will be rewarded not only by the spectacular views, but also by a truly handsome certificate, awarded by the resort at dinner, attesting to your feat.

Take out one of the sturdy six-passenger motor boats. There is no charge. They have good sized outboard engines and were among the most substantial dinghies we were offered at any resort. Except when the winds are particularly strong, these boats will get you most almost anywhere around the island, or even across to Palfrey Island where the lighthouse is situated, or to other parts of the Blue Lagoon. Some of the best skin diving in the world is to be found between Palfrey and South Islands, weather permitting.

The Blue Lagoon, almost as big in area as the land mass of the island itself, is bounded by the south shore and the sweeping coral reef. Palfrey Island is at the west edge, South Island at the south point of the lagoon, and Bird Islets at the east edge just next to the lagoon entrance. From the shore, you can make out the presence of several subreefs within the bay. Viewed from above, the reef activity is nothing short of spectacular.There is an amazing variety of color and depth to the water.This is a must visit, probably more than once during your stay on Lizard.

While you are here, you can fish from the dinghies inside the reef, right in the bay in front of the resort if you wish. Other activities include swimming, water skiing, wind surfing, aqua scooter, a new swimming pool, and the glass bottom boat.

THE GREAT BARRIER REEF

There is an island barbecue lunch on one of the nearby beaches on Thursdays to which most hotel guests go. Any time you request, the kitchen will also prepare a cold picnic lunch or barbecue for you to take to one of the many secluded beaches, or to a nearby island on the fringing reef.

There are two or three pleasant walks through the island national park, and it is possible to visit the Research Station around the point from the resort. On Tuesdays and Fridays at 4:00 p.m. the staff of the station puts on a slide show and explains their work on the island. Of course, you can also lie around and just relax in the chaises on the great lawn overlooking the beautiful beach or by the new pool, but you may find with so many activities available that you have little time left.

It probably wasn't too hard for you to notice our enthusiasm for this island, which many people consider their favorite in the Great Barrier Reef region and beyond. We certainly didn't mind that the resort does not have a direct telephone line – not even for the resort itself. Calls must be routed by marine radio-telephone from OTC out of Townsville or by telex through the booking office in Cairns, which has a private cable line only with this resort.

Air Queensland was an original part owner of this facility; with TAA's takeover of the airline, they now become a principle in this resort as well. We sincerely hope they remain the silent partner that Air Queensland has been. Why tamper with such a successful formula?

Due to its location, a trip to Lizard most likely will be the beginning or climax to your sojourn to these island resorts.

However, because it is so far off the beaten track (even for Great Barrier Reef hotels), is so popular with fishing parties and has such exclusive accommodations, it is probably wise to invest the $10 or $15 dollars in a direct telephone call to Air Queensland in Cairns when you are first planning your Australia itinerary to see whether this pleasant and hospitable island will be able to accept your reservation.

Lizard Island Lodge
Private Bag 40
Post Office
Cairns, Qld. 4870
Air Queensland [70] 504 310

Reservations through Air Queensland, or Dive-in Australia, 680 Beach Street, Suite 498, San Francisco, California 94109; telephone [415] 928-4480 or [800] 227-5436, **or** GWF Marketing, 60 East 42nd Street, Room1504 New York, New York 10165 telephone [212] 697-3694 or [800] 221-3041

on Lizard Island

on Long Island

LONG

• coral viewing • national park • bushwalks
• fishing • waterskiing • anchorage • tennis • golf
• sailing • snorkeling • windsurfing • swimming

THE GREAT BARRIER REEF

Thick, undisturbed rain forest covers most of this pretty island. It is one of the larger in the Whitsunday Group and the only island, other than Magnetic to the north, to have more than one distinct overnight facility. Long is the closest resort island to the coast, visible at night, located just about five miles southeast of Shute Harbor. The island forms a beautiful passage for the coastal sail from Shute Harbor south into the Whitsunday group.

Until a year or so ago, **Happy Bay Resort** toward the northern end of Long Island, was a quietly popular family resort, a favorite among many local residents. Then, suddenly a new group of entrepreneurs obtained a sublease and converted the resort to **Whitsunday 100**, and their brochures announce the resort is for *18 - 35's* (they don't permit children under 18) and that their swinging scene will make Great Keppel Island seem as tame as a *vicarage tea party*. Based on our inspection we would lower that upper age range somewhat, but the idea here is clear: *this resort is definitely for the young in mind.* Rumor has it that the resort actually turned away a wealthy Australian notable when he radioed from his yacht for reservations, but admitted to being over thirty! A visit, however, confirms what locals whisper: the idea isn't working very well.

The resort is reached by daily launch from Shute Harbor ($A7 each way; about 20 minutes) or connection with flights in and out of Hamilton Island ($A10 each way; 35 minutes). Helicopter service is available from Proserpine, but must be arranged. There are day trips possible from Shute Harbor ($A21) which include launch, lunch and use of the recreation facilities.

Cabins face the beachfront. There are blocks of one-story units, and some ever-so-slightly-larger free-standing bungalows ($A69 per person per night, meals included with wine with lunch and dinner), all rather reminiscent of college dormitory facilities. As with other Barrier Reef resorts, there is a standby rate ($A50 including transfers; $A98 two night, three day stand-by) for guests reserving less than 48 hours prior to arrival, and accepting multi-occupancy accommodations on an as-available basis. Units have showers, refrigerators, ceiling fans, tea and coffee making facility, double and day beds, and little else.

on Long Island

THE GREAT BARRIER REEF

The dining room and cocktail lounge desperately need a decorator's touch. (Actually, that's true of most of the resort!) In the reception area, one finds the *Ripoff Shop*. Honestly, that's what they call it. Nearby there is a barbecue area, a recreation area and dance hall.

Activities include windsurfing, catamarans, surf skis, snorkeling, water skiing, dinghies, fishing, tennis on an obviously only occasionally maintained compressed clay/sand court, ping pong, and lots of *everyone into the pool for volley ball*. Room rates include use of all sporting and marine equipment. Scuba, paraflying, day cruises and reef flights are extra. There are also lots of signs around telling you how to recover from the *morning after* effects of the night before. The resort advertises *the best resort beach in the Whitsunday Passage*. Regrettably, the beach becomes a swamp at low tide. We left our dinghy too far up on the sand and strained many muscles and all patience getting it back to the water line which quickly retreated as the tide went out.

Extracts from their recent brochure, reveal a great deal about **Whitsunday 100.**

- *If the pace doesn't flatten you, a falling coconut probably will.*
- *The island where some people actually manage to do it standing up.*
- *The island where some people prefer to do it sitting down.*
- *The island where there are 3 girls for every boy.*
- *The island where there are 3 boys for every girl.*
- *The island where D. J. means Discovered in the Jungle.*

Whitsunday 100 may appeal to some, but more likely it will remind you of the college beer bust that got entirely out of hand.

A twenty-minute walk south from **Whitsunday 100** along a well-marked path brings you to **Palm Bay**, a very small do-it-yourself camp, with very low cost accommodations ($A46.50 per cabin). These are cabins with minimal amenities. Units have cooking facilities, communal showers and toilets close by. The island shop, part of the management/reception cabin, is moderately well stocked so you can prepare your own meals. **Palm Bay** is one step above camping and allows you to be in a beautiful part of the world and enjoy the water. And you're far enough from **Whitsunday 100** that you may be able to ignore it entirely.

Whitsunday 100
Long Island, Qld. 4800
telephone [79] 469 400

Reservations through Ansett

Palm Bay Resort
Palm Bay
Long Island, Qld. 4800
telephone [79] 469 233

Reservations direct to the resort.

a school of fish just below the surface of the water

LOW ISLETS

- no resort • day trips • densely forested
- coral atolls

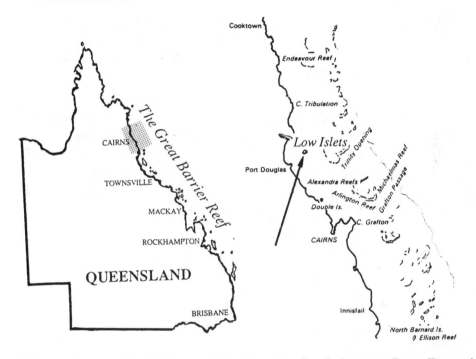

Every day at 10:30 the M.V. Martin Cash leaves Port Douglas Wharf for the brief trip to Low Islets. These tiny, yet densely forested coral atolls, have long been A favorite day trip of those familiar with the Barrier Reef The only permanent residents of this tiny isle are the lighthouse keepers and their families, and there are no overnight hotel or resort facilities. What makes this trip a favorite is the close proximity to major portions of the Barrier Reef, allowing some of the best snorkeling and coral viewing in northern Queensland. There is also a glass bottom boat. Those with rubber shoes can generally walk right from the beach onto at least part of the reef, weather and tides permitting.

THE GREAT BARRIER REEF

The day trip ($A26 per person, or $A32 including round trip bus service from Cairns) includes smorgasbord luncheon, morning and afternoon tea and snack, and the use of snorkel gear and glass bottom boat. If by any chance you have kitchen facilities available where you are staying, you might be interested in joining the locals buying fresh fish from the fishing boats that sell part of their daily catch to the lighthouse keepers and their families, and the day visitors to Low Islets.

The boat returns to Port Douglas at 4:30 p.m., in plenty of time to permit easy return to Cairns in ample time for dinner.

For further information or advance reservations contact Maritime World, 2618 Newport Blvd., Newport Beach, California 92633; telephone [714] 675-2250.

Lizard Island

MAGNETIC

- coral viewing • national park • bushwalks
- fishing • scuba diving • anchorage • tennis
- golf • sailing • snorkeling • windsurfing
- swimming • horseback riding

THE GREAT BARRIER REEF

Named by Captain Cook in 1770 because his cOmpass appeared to be influenced by the island while the *Endeavor* was near it. In fact, the island is not *magnetic*, although it does possess substantial deposits of the mineral magnetite, which will affect the old astrolabe compass. Seventy percent of the island is a national park and bird sanctuary. The terrain is hilly and rocky. There are several very pleasant bays, particularly the very photogenic *Arthur Bay,* with interesting rock formations. There are also koala, rock wallabies and numerous birds. The national park has several well graded walking trails.

Like Green Island, Magnetic was first served in 1899 by the Butler Family who started ferry service. This is a fairly large continental island and is the biggest of the northern islands. It is in reality not a resort island, but an island of resorts. In addition, it is a suburb of Townsville, just five miles off the coast, where many people live and commute daily to the city. Magnetic is reached by vehicular ferry and ten or so daily Hayles Cruises launch services ($A5.50 round trip) or by Rundle Air Service or helicopter from Townsville ($A40 each way). You can sail to Magnetic (the anchorage is at Picnic Bay at the south end), but it is a poor location for overnight mooring.

The several village-like areas are linked by roads, with bus and taxi service available. There is a fairly extensive network of sealed roads. The eastern shoreline is developed; the rest of the island is readily accessible wilderness. In all, there are five populated bays with tourist facilities.

Accommodations range from hotel/motel units to self-contained flats. These resorts, unlike much of the Barrier Reef area, are part of developed freehold properties, and are not on lease. There are two hotels; three holiday resorts; numerous motels, guest houses, holiday flats, hostels, and camping areas. Both the **Hotel Magnetic** and **Hotel Arcadia** have bars, dining rooms, snack bars, fresh water swimming pools, and are close to the beach and the island's two landing points. (both $A35-70 per unit without meals). There is also the **Mediterranean Holiday Village** with rooms with showers, air conditioning, TV and radio, piped music, tea or coffee maker, refrigerator, licensed restaurants, cocktail lounges, two tennis courts, swimming pool, beauty salon, boutique, golf, fishing, biking and boating, island cruises. In all ,there are a dozen licensed restaurants and several bars and cafes.

At *Horseshoe Bay,* you can visit the *Oasis Koala Park* ($A4 per person) where injured koalas are cared for and are very approachable; otherwise this is not a particular interesting zoo. You can swim in this bay, but watch for the many shark nets set around it. Check with staff to see if there is any shark danger. Probably the nicest park and beach is at *Alma Bay.* There is also a *Marine Garden* and, at *Melly Bay, Shark World.* The island offers golf, tennis, paddle boats, and catamarans, as well as shops and rental cars, Mini-Mokes, push bikes and motorcycles.

For further information contact the Queensland Tourist and Travel Corp., 3550 Wilshire Blvd., Los Angeles, California 90010; telephone [213] 381-3062

on Long Island

NEWRY

• cabins for campers • fishing • oystering
• koala sanctuary

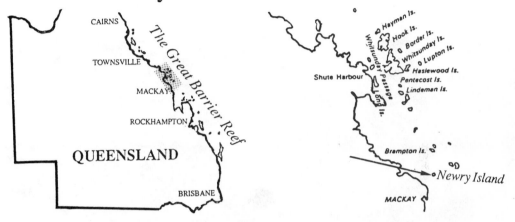

Located 34 miles north of Mackay, Newry is south of Brampton and, in a peripheral and rather remote sense, part of the Whitsunday Passage group of islands. It is reached by a pick-up boat which leaves from Victor Creek, Seaforth near Mackay ($A5 round trip), at 11:00 a.m. and 4:00 p.m. for the fifteen minute trip. The island boasts excellent fishing and a particularly abundant supply of oysters. It also has a koala sanctuary. There is a very small unpretentious facility consisting of self-contained cabins for campers – that is, with little in the way of services, but a comparably low price ($A30 per person per day, double occupancy, full board; $A20 per person room only). Units sleep a maximum of five people, and some have cooking facilities.

Fishing and oystering are the most popular activities and there is some water skiing. There is no nightlife, but there is a fully licensed bar open all hours, with meals and snacks available.

For further information telephone [79] 590 214.

on Orpheus Island

ORPHEUS

- coral viewing • national park • bushwalks
- fishing • waterskiing • scuba diving • tennis
- golf • sailing • snorkeling • windsurfing
- swimming

THE GREAT BARRIER REEF

This is a relatively long, narrow island, about six miles by 1/2 mile. Largely a national park, it is located roughly 50 miles northeast of Townsville. Part of the Palm Islands group, it is 15 miles off shore and within sight of the mainland, near Hinchinbrook Channel, and six or seven miles south of the southern end of Hinchinbrook. Orpheus is about nine miles from the outer Barrier Reef. It was named in 1887 by a British Admiralty surveyor, to commemorate a ship wrecked two decades earlier off new Zealand, with the loss of all hands, including the commander-in-chief of the Australia Station.

As with many other islands along the Great Barrier Reef chain, provisions were placed for lost or shipwrecked mariners. Today 400 wild goats still survive as part of this history. There are also remnants of stone sheep pens, dating back to early in the century. The island has been used for commercial oystering as well. At the south end of *Hazard Bay,* south of the beach occupied by the resort, cement pilings remain from a degaussing or demagnetizing station used for submarines during World War II. Here one finds the best snorkeling beach on the island. The present ownership bought the island in 1980 and, after two years of planning and complete renovation, opened the resort just before Christmas in 1981.

Geographically the island presents different faces. Volcanic in design, parts appear relatively dry, while around the next point you will find a lush beach interrupted with a stand of mangrove trees. There are numerous points around the island with large boulders scattered interestingly, and there are abundant pisonia and palm trees. Beaches are generally sandy, although in some areas the inshore coral has died, leaving exposed flats at very low tides. The beaches are relatively shallow, however, and taper nicely into the lagoon, so they are among the best in the tropics for swimming, splashing around, water sports and easy snorkeling.

We found this to be a very sophisticated and elegant resort, particularly for such a small independent operation. It is a hideaway for adults. Families with children are occasionally accepted on a very selective basis. **Orpheus'** affable and conscientious manager, Paul Roberts, sails out with the launch to greet your seaplane. After you register, he escorts you to your room or bungalow, where a complimentary large cold island punch (containing ample doses of three different rums) awaits you on your coffee table.

Orpheus is most usually reached by Air Whitsunday 13-passenger seaplane service aboard Grumman twin engine high wing aircraft Wednesday, Saturday and Sunday ($A70 each way). Interestingly, because Hinchinbrook Island is so close to the north, this flight also serves that island, giving these two barrier reef island resorts the almost unique distinction of being linked directly by air. This might be important if you have travelled eight thousand miles for a holiday and would appreciate some convenience in getting from one resort to another, instead of having to return to the mainland.

A very expensive helicopter charter ($A400 each way), carrying a maximum of four passengers, is also available. One couple we were told about, chartered an Air Whitsunday plane to pick them up in Cairns and deposit them directly in the waters off Orpheus for a mere $A3000.

There are also launches from Townsville or Dungeness, near Ingham or from Lucinda Point on the coast opposite, but prices are somewhat high because of the small numbers of people making the passage.The real problem of getting transportation to Lucinda discourages most people. For now, access is realistically through Townsville. There is no deep anchorage available close to shore for boats because of the shallow low tides. Indeed, even the resort must moor its larger boats well away from the beach. In addition, to insure the privacy of the guests and maintain the level of the operation, management discourages visits from yachties without special prior arrangements.

The island lodge accommodates but twenty-five couples (families with children accepted only by special arrangement with management) in recently thoroughly renovated and redecorated rooms. The open air lounge is beautifully tropical with high ceiling, open sides to allow the tropical breezes to flow through, an elegant blend of tropical wood, rattan and blue fabric. It is well situated to take advantage of the view of ocean and distant coastline.*Tea* (that is, coffee and tea and, in the afternoon, sweet cookies) is served British fashion at eleven and four. The room has an elegant comfort and openness about it. Similarly, the adjacent dining commons is open on three sides, has many overhead fans, and a large, attractive and well maintained tropical fish tank for decoration. It is elegantly, yet very simply appointed. Drinks are served on silver trays by what the British would undoubtedly call a *properly attired barman.*

There are two types of studios ($A140 per person per day, all meals included; very stiff single supplement to single price $A210 per day), grouped four to a building in single story beachfront buildings set inconspicuously into their surroundings. These handsome accommodations, some done in wood and stucco, with white tile floors, and others in more Mediterranean style, with white stucco and mixed sand and white floor tiles, have double bed and day sofa with ample space for bed and sitting area, cooled by an overhead fan, spacious tile shower and separate vanity area, refrigerator with mini bar, tea and coffee-making facilities, and a sound system to bring you local radio stations and music. The decor is bright tropical.

There are two bungalow units ($A320 per couple per day) which are luxurious, larger detached beachfront units, have queen size beds, without a day bed, but with a lovely conversation area. Floors are large squares of terra cotta tile. Rooms have ample windows, French doors, potted green plants and yellow orange drapes. Walls are grass cloth, except for the one of polished dark wood strips set on the diagonal behind the bed. The furniture is handsome wood and rattan. The special feature of the bungalows is a large beautifully appointed tiled *tropical garden bathroom* , with french doors opening onto a tiny private garden and an extravagant four-foot diameter sunken bath tub with shower.

The resort provides luxury soaps, face creams, bath oils, extra towels for the beach and at poolside, without your asking, and such necessities as a sewing kit, shower cap, insect repellent, hand laundry cream soap. Also provided are free copies of the fine waterproof edition of the pamphlet *Introductory Guide to Life on the Great Barrier Reef* , published by the Great Barrier Reef Marine Park Authority. This ingenious publication is designed so you can actually take it underwater while you are snorkeling, to compare photos with the real marine world, and read brief explanations about what you are seeing.

Fine tropical dining, said one travel brochure. We'll go further. For a tropical resort, especially one with such a small clientele (remember they can only accommodate fifty people), the resort has a gifted kitchen, which we learned had just been placed in the hands of the gentleman who had been working as the under-chef. All three meals are á la carte and served.

Breakfasts are English style and far too generous for most of us: fish, meats, omelettes, eggs, fruits, cereals, etc., etc., etc. For lunch and dinner, two or three selections are offered, depending upon the number of guests at the resort. Generally the choice is a local fish or a meat or fowl dish. Sauces are offered with the advice that you can ask for any variation you may desire. The chef is quite willing to prepare food to your taste. The wine list is of good quality, but with an emphasis on the higher price selections. It is a tad more abbreviated than one might hope for, but this is perhaps understandable given the difficulties of warehousing wines in the tropics, the small number of consumers, and the level of quality the resort obviously strives to maintain. The house wines served from the bar are quite pleasant, can be ordered by glass ($A1.50) or carafe ($A8), and just as important, both red and white house wines were correctly cared for so they did not become stale and oxidized from the heat.

Dinner was always exciting. Prawns steamed perfectly with an exquisite spicy chili sauce were offered as an entree (remember again, entree means introductory course in Australia), but on this evening the dish made a perfect main course for a hot summer evening – one which prompted us to ask for the recipe. For a simpler meal, a filet done exactly as ordered, tender as the finest U.S. beef, served with a boqueterie of perfectly cooked fresh vegetables with a light butter sauce. Another evening's barramundi (an Australian coastal river fish, generally considered their finest) was superb. The fried scallops with a lemon buttersauce were simple and excellent. The emphasis throughout is on fresh local foods, including tropical fruits and seafood.

Lunches are equally appropriate and properly handled. Cold soup or entree and fish or meat, followed by a small, pleasant fruit and cheese table was the menu for one day. The resort also proudly features its picnic lunches for you to take wherever you might desire on this small island. At the specified time, a large cooler chest is loaded aboard a small motor boat, and you may select your own spot for a totally private picnic on a secluded beach. Or, should you prefer to be chauffeured, one of the staff will deposit you by boat on your secluded paradise, and pick you up at the appointed hour.

The staff is well coached and very pleasant. Service is attentive and pleasant, but not offensively, professional. Unfortunately, this island, as with all of the smaller vacation resorts, experiences a fairly high turnover of staff. Thus the continuation of the high standards depends upon competent management in the training of personnel as they are added, and **Orpheus** definitely seems to have that. It is evident that every effort is made to set and maintain an elegant level of polite service.

The resort has one nicely maintained astro-turf tennis court which they service weekly to keep in good shape. They also have a lovely small swimming pool with ocean view, and a hot tub, which didn't have much appeal during the ninety degree heat which lasted throughout our stay. Catamaran, sailing, windsurfing, paddle boards, outboard powered dinghies, snorkeling equipment, and glass bottom viewing boat are all included in the price. This relatively small island has seven secluded bays and beaches. For fees quite comparable to those on other islands (beginning at $A40 per person), you can cruise to the Outer

Reef (always, weather and tides permitting), take fishing trips, charter a speedboat with a driver, or cruise aboard the 30' ketch *Freckled Duck* or 40' cruiser *Orpheus*.

Orpheus Island boasts some of the best coral in the entire Barrier Reef region. The surrounding waters are so rich in marine life that James Cook University has established a *Marine Research Station* in a quiet area of the island. Like other Barrier Reef islands, Orpheus is also well known for its abundant supply of birds. At least 50 species have been identified.

If the tide is low, the staff urge you to take a motorboat or catamaran and sail to their float in the middle of their peaceful bay, from which the snorkeling is excellent right in front of the resort, or to try the bay two beaches to the south, where there is abundant live coral near the pilings marking the old submarine mooring spot. If you are planning an afternoon of swimming, sunning or snorkeling on the float, ask the office for the portable two-way radio to take to the raft. Should you become thirsty, you need only call the bar, and the barman will promptly deliver your beverage order by motorboat to the float.

Dress is casual, although the resort invites you to dress up if you wish. You may find the surroundings so elegant that you will want to. The brochure in your room advises that *we do ask that swimsuits be the minimum dress. For those who wish to get an all over tan, we'll be happy to take you to one of our secluded beaches.* There is a tiny boutique which sells toiletries as well as souvenirs. Commercial laundry service is available.There is only one telephone line to the island, so guests are requested to keep calls to three minutes.Telephone use is limited to office hours. The staff will book your on-going Air Whitsunday flights for you. You can add them to your bill, thereby enabling you to put them on a credit card if you are not already ticketed.

Orpheus is where Australian movie stars and visiting British nobility go to relax in the tropics. It is an island for couples who enjoy being alone, and the resort sets a tone not found on other Barrier Reef island. This is by no means an inexpensive island, although when you consider all of the activities and amenities included in the price, the load is lightened somewhat. In reality, Orpheus can cost you half-again as much as other resorts. Indeed, Orpheus does bill itself as *The Exclusive Barrier Reef Resort,* but then again it may be that you are ready for some totally rewarding self-indulgence.

Orpheus Island Resort
Private Mail Bag
Ingham, Qld. 4850

[77] 777 377

Reservations direct to the resort or Pacific Insight Marketing, 2618 Newport Blvd., Newport Beach, California 92663; telephone [714] 675-2250 or, from within California, [800] 282-1402; outside of California [800] 282-1401

PALM

- aborigine reservation
permission needed to visit

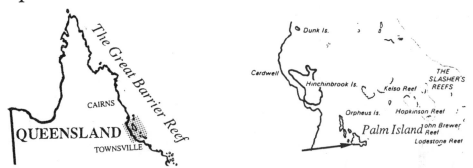

Located thirty-six miles northwest of Townsville, this continental island is the largest in the Palm group. It was named by Captain Cook, who landed there and found it was inhabited by a tribe of native Australians. In 1918 the Australian government established a *mission* or reservation for Aborigines. The island is governed by an indigenous council, and is financed and administered by the Department of Aboriginal and Island Advancement. The population is about 1300.

Except for Orpheus Island just to the north, all islands in the Palm group are part of the Aboriginal reserve and cannot be visited without special permission from the governmental agency administering the mission. Contact must first be made with officials in Brisbane,Townsville, or directly with the island manager, to obtain permission to use the landing strip or the island.

Fantome Island, in this group, was a leper colony until 1974. All of the buildings were then razed by fire, and the remaining inhabitants removed to a hospital on Palm Island.

sailing near South Molle Island

RAINE

• no tourist facilities • sea turtle rookery

Situated off Cape Grenville, north of Lizard Island, this is the world's largest rookery. Between November and February as many as 16,000 turtles crowd the island to lay eggs. There are no tourist facilities on the island.

on South Molle Island

SOUTH MOLLE

- coral viewing • national park • bushwalks
- fishing • waterskiing • scuba diving
- anchorage • tennis • golf • sailing • snorkeling
- windsurfing • swimming

THE GREAT BARRIER REEF

North Molle is for camping, West Molle is better known as Daydream, and there is no East Molle. South Molle, in the middle of Whitsunday Passage, is roughly sixty miles north of Mackay and five miles from Shute Harbor. Until late 1984 it was the largest island resort of the Whitsunday Group, when it was outstripped by both Hamilton and Hayman Islands. Hilly, covered with grassland, native trees and pockets of rain forest, this national park is fringed with palm trees, with a coast punctuated with numerous bays, inlets and coral gardens, and surrounded by fringing coral reefs.There are bush walks with panoramic views from *Mt. Jeffreys* and *Spion Kop*. There is abundant bird life, and the lorikeets (small multi-colored parrots) are fed daily next to the tennis courts. South Molle, one of the most scenic in the Whitsundays, is a large island with good walking paths and good hilltop views across the Whitsunday Passage overlooking Hayman, Hook and Whitsunday Islands, among others.

The giant high-speed Telford South Molle catamaran carries guests to the resort daily from Shute Harbor ($A10) or from the jet airstrip at Hamilton Island on Wednesdays, Saturdays and Sundays, meeting the in-coming Ansett flight from Melbourne, Sidney and Brisbane. Helicopter service can still be arranged from Mackay via Ansett 26 passenger Sikorsky helicopter, taking 45 minutes ($A59 per person) or from Proserpine (slightly lower fare), but this has become the less used way to reach this resort. There are ten boat moorings for visiting yachts ($A20 per day).

South Molle Island Resort is a village style collection of bungalows and multi-unit buildings, set in tropical gardens overlooking Bauer Bay. It features a casual, relaxed atmosphere, and its activities are centered around a newly remodeled pool complex. There are currently seven categories of accommodations totaling 202 rooms. Units are generally wood panelled and not luxury accommodations by U.S. standards. They are somewhat small and old fashioned, but very clean and equipped with ample amenities.

Whitsunday units ($A90 per person per day, double occupancy, including all meals) are on the beach and have queen size and single beds, bath tubs as well as showers, fan and air conditioning, telephones, refrigerators, color television, tea or coffee making facilities, and refrigerators. **Polynesian units** ($A85) are uphill, perhaps 200 yards from the main complex, and have a lovely northern view of the bay and, except for bath tubs and tile floors, similar appointments to the Whitsunday rooms.

The **Reef Lodge** ($A85) consists of motel style units in back of the Whitsunday group. These pleasant rooms face the golf course, rather than the beach, are simpler than the others, and have black and white television. There are fifteen Reef Lodge units equipped for family use with a pull partition to divide the room in two, with singles and bunks for four children. **Balamara units** ($A80) are on the beach. These are the only units predating the take-over of this resort by the Telford hotel chain. These separate cabins have water view, double and single beds, patio or deck, color TV and the same appointments as the other units.They are older and show their age, which is why they are priced slightly lower in spite of the good location. They are to be rebuilt in the near future ,no doubt with a substantial price increase to reflect the upgrading.

Like many other Whitsunday area resorts, South Molle offers a stand-by rate ($A40 single, $A60 per couple) for guests reserving less than 48 hours before their arrival and accepting accommodations on an as available basis.

The **Whitehouse Lodge** and **Sealife Lodge** are separate facilities, generally for those who have been camping in the area, have their own bedding (usually sleeping bags), and wish to stay at a resort island. Both offer bunk beds, laundry, shared toilet facilities, and a communal kitchen. **Whitehouse Lodge** has six units built around a central courtyard in a garden setting; **Sealife Lodge** has eleven dormitory style rooms, intended for young singles, with two bunk beds, dressing table, ceiling fan in each room. The principal difference between **Whitehouse** and **Sealife Lodges** is that the latter does not specifically cater to organized groups. Both charge nominal tariffs, but do not provide meals in the resort restaurants. Camping is permitted in designated portions of the island.

Meals are served in a large, air-conditioned dining area, done in bamboo wood and green plastic, located at the base of the U-shaped complex surrounding the large swimming pool. Lunch is a routine self-service buffet. The kitchen shows little inspiration. Fortunately, there is a pianist who plays nightly during dinner. The Friday night buffet dinner is a vast spread which, among other dishes, includes a huge offering of fresh regional fish and shell fish. This highly regarded smorgasbord is touted throughout the Whitsunday area. The Telford ferry runs a special *booze cruise* on Fridays (the *Island Feast Night cruise*, $A30 all inclusive) to take people from Shute Harbor to South Molle for dinner, remaining on for the *south seas* cabaret, and returning via a sweeping tour of the north-central Whitsunday Passage around midnight.

The *Coral Room* is an á la carte seafood restaurant, open only for dinner. It is considerably smaller and much more attractive than the main dining area. There is an additional charge for dinners here, however. The wine list for both main dining room and the restaurant is ample and contains many good selections in the $A8-12 range, which is considerably more modest than many of the other Barrier Reef resorts.

The entertainment center is a vast dark barn of a room filled with cocktail tables and plastic chairs. This cavern triples as a conference center, game room, and evening bar/cabaret to showcase the resident band. It does boast two very large murals by a local artist, one of Captain Cook and the other of his ship the *Endeavor*. Regrettably, the lighting is so poor in the room that the murals are probably only noticed by ten percent or less of the visitors to the resort.

Evening activities, aside from the resident band, include discos, dress-up frolics, amateur nights, bingo, and toad and crab racing. As indicated earlier, most of the rooms have television, and there is a large screen TV in the game room section of the entertainment center.

There are coin-operated laundry facilities, banking and postal office, highchairs and cots for children, and an island photographer.The island store was, in our estimation, significantly understocked for a resort of this size. The small arcade of shops includes a small diving store, hairdresser, laundry, and snack bar.

South Molle possesses a beautiful nine-hole golf course and has a resident professional. Clubs are $A3 for half day rental, and balls and tees are available for purchase. There are two paved all-weather tennis courts with lights for night playing, and there

THE GREAT BARRIER REEF

is no charge for court time. (Tennis rackets, however, are $A2.50 per hour!) There is a squash court (rackets $A1.50 per half hour), free archery, a gymnasium with a spa and sauna, volleyball, ping pong, badminton. lawn bowling, billiards, pin ball machines, beach cricket and softball games. There are also separate programs for children, including wading pool, playground, game room and the like. Children are supervised free of charge in the nursery from 6:00 p.m. to 9:00 p.m. nightly to permit parents to have dinner alone. At other times, baby sitting is available by off-duty hotel staff at normal rates.

The water sports are ample, but almost everything carries an extra charge. Free equipment *is* available for paddle skiing and snorkeling.There are water bicycles ($A6 per half hour), windsurfers ($A6 per hour), maricats for sailing ($A10 per hour, but this at least includes instruction), parasailing ($A20 per ride, also including instruction), water skiing ($A6 without instruction, $A10 with), and dinghies with five horsepower motors ($A10 per hour).The island offers scuba instruction ($A45 for an introductory course; $A250 for the full five day PADI accredited course). Fishing is available off the jetty ($A2 to rent a fishing rod, $A1 for a hand line) and you can buy bait.

There are day and half-day cruises visiting Daydream, Hayman, Long, Lindeman, Dent, or Hamilton among other destinations (beginning at $A20). Weather and tides permitting, there are day cruises to the outer reef ($A50 to $A90). Telford owns a float and moored submarine at the outer reef, which permit visitors to get a real close-up view.Scuba equipment is available for rent ($A25). The resort runs nearby boat trips for diving ($A25 per person for scuba or snorkelers) and outer reef dive trips ($A40 per person).

This resort is owned by the Telford Hotel chain, an Australian operation with resorts and hotels across the country. Telford also owns the observatory at Hook Island ($A5), and trips to the underwater viewing rooms are offered frequently.

Unfortunately, after a series of real estate investment setbacks, Telford is now in an Australian form of receivership, and its properties are being operated by trustees. What this will mean to renovation plans for South Molle is hard to say, but the resort does continue to operate and enjoy a fine reputation in its own right.

South Molle may not offer the most exciting rooms or food, but it does have one of the most complete activities program for a resort of its size. Many long-time residents of the Whitsunday area rank this resort very high on their list.

Telford South Molle Island Resort
via Proserpine, Qld. 4800
[79] 469 433

Reservations through Telford Hotels, 881 Alma Real Drive, Suite 314, Pacific Palisades, California 90272; telephone [213] 459-2691 or, from within California [800] 833-3374, and outside of California [800] 445-5505

Whitsunday Island

WHITSUNDAY

• national park • no resort • beach camping

THE GREAT BARRIER REEF

This very large island national park, biggest of the islands in the group to which it gives its name, is the center of a group of resort and uninhabited islands off Proserpine, about midway along the Queensland coast. Captain Cook landed here in 1770, naming the island for the day on which he set foot there. Markers at Cid Harbor, on the west coast of the island, commemorate the landing.

Whitsunday Island has no resort, although camping is permitted on the island at several beach points. The island itself is too densely forested to permit much interior trekking, except by the hardiest hiker/backpacker. Cid Harbor offers a good anchorage to sail and power boats, as well as a very pretty beach. By small boat you can reach some smaller even prettier beaches just around the bend to the north of Cid. On the southeast side of the island, Turtle Bay is a particularly interesting and attractive anchorage.

The Whitsunday Passage separates the islands of the Whitsunday group (Hook, Whitsunday, Border, Haslewood, Hamilton, Dent and Cid) from the main land. Daydream, South Molle, Pine and Long Islands lie offshore. There are seventy-four islands within the Whitsunday, and just to the south, Cumberland groups, many virtually uninhabited. Day cruises ($A30) are available to Whitehaven Beach from Shute Harbor on board the *Hamilton Quick Cat,* a large modern high-speed catamaran.

The resort islands arrayed to the north, west and south (no resorts to the east) around Whitsunday are (counter-clockwise from the north) Hayman, Day dream, South Molle, Long (Whitsunday 100 and Palm Bay camping cabins), Hamilton and Lindeman. The under water observatory on Hook Island (owned and operated by Telford South Molle Resort) is just across the narrow channel separating northern Whitsunday from Hook. If you are in the Whitsunday Passage, Hook Island is particularly worth a visit even though it has no resort, because it offers the *best scuba diving and snorkeling in the area.*

Islands near Whitsunday

downtown Brisbane

COASTAL CITIES and TOWNS

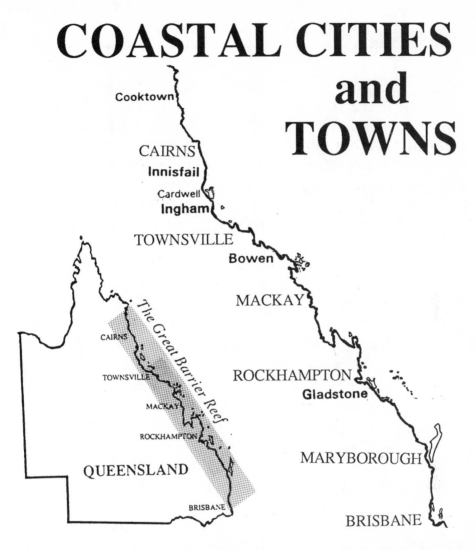

The North Queensland coastline is *itself* a growing vacation land. All of the cities and towns along the way are now advertising resorts, and indeed many of them show great promise. This is an old and fiercely independent part of Australia, and people here live much as they did fifty years ago. Since you inevitably will spend at least some time in and around gateway cities (the airports are generally but a few minutes taxi ride from the center of town), we thought some information about them, and their sister towns, would be interesting.

THE GREAT BARRIER REEF

Brisbane (*BRIZ-bn* to locals) calls itself the Gateway City, and for many it is the first stop in the northerly tour to the Great Barrier Reef ,or the climax of the southerly journey through Queensland. Geographically, this capitol of the State of Queensland, is the third largest city in the world, incorporating a huge area within a single city limits, although its population is just under a million. It is an international port for Qantas, with service by both national jet airlines and several feeder carriers, and with regular bus and rail traffic. The city is favored by temperate climate virtually throughout the year, and so is base city for the nearby Gold Coast to the south and less developed, but increasingly popular, Sunshine Coast, to the north.

Taxi fare in from the airport should be under $10, and the trip ordinarily is only twenty minutes or so, unless at rush hour, or when the roads are congested for some other reason. If you find yourself in Brisbane for a day or so, the downtown area is very compact, easily toured on foot, and is definitely cosmopolitan, with a colorful mix of modern highrise interspersed with old, small brightly-painted Victorian and Edwardian buildings. A two block strip of Queen Street, in the main shopping area, has been closed to vehicle traffic to form a delightful mall (here pronounced like the *a* in *pal*). At either end there are outdoor restaurants, both called *Jimmy's At the Mall* . At one end fish dishes are served, and at the other meat and diverse lunches. The *Brisbane Visitors Bureau* is situated in a kiosk at the Albert Street end of the mall, and people there are very gracious and helpful with shopping, restaurant, touring and other advice for travelers.

The City Hall on King George Square, just a block from the mall, is a dramatic Edwardian-style stone building with marble interior and a tall clock tower. Behind the City Hall is a small square with several shops (including a large news agency) and restaurants. We particularly enjoyed *Agatha Christie's* – an elegant recreation of an Orient Express dining car. It is open for lunch and dinner.

Incidentally, we found that you can check things until 10:00 p.m., for 45 cents, at the cloak room in the ladies' lounge in the side basement of the City Hall, with its separate entrance on Adelaide Street. This is very convenient if you find yourself with a long day between flights, or otherwise want to park your bags, especially since only the domestic air terminal in Brisbane has lockers. The international terminal where Qantas lands does not.

Cairns

THE GREAT BARRIER REEF

The brief tour of Brisbane should include the short walk down George, Albert or Edward Streets to Alice Street to see the attractive *Botanic Gardens*. With the interesting *Parliament House* and other public buildings nearby, and with its pleasant tailored grounds, this is a most handsome public city park. Bicycles may be rented on Margaret Street, near the Parkroyal Hotel for riding in the Gardens, and there are snack trucks near the bandstand area. The Gardens are bordered on three sides by the Brisbane River, and the river bank is a pleasant setting for watching the boats, or perhaps for a picnic. The *Edward Street ferry* runs from the edge of the Gardens back and forth across the river every ten minutes or so.

For those spending a bit more time in the area, the *Lone Pine Koala Sanctuary* is one of the most popular attractions. About a forty-five minute bus ride from the center of town (considerably shorter by rental a car or taxi), this animal park permits close up visits with kangaroos and koalas, and a chance to observe emus, wombats and even the shy platypus.

Brisbane, of course, has many large and small hotels. In earlier days the *Parkroyal* was the favorite, but more recently local residents speak highly of the new *Sheraton* built atop the rail station. The brand new *Hilton* expects to draw a large portion of visitor interest as well. Even if your program does not call for overnighting in Brisbane, this city can be enjoyed with a brief visit. If your travel schedule allows, you may want to arrange part of a day to enjoy this urbane combination of nineteenth and twentieth centuries.

Cairns likes to call itself the *Gateway to the Great Barrier Reef.* Now that Quantas has inaugurated non-stop service from the West Coast, the sobriquet is probably more true than ever. Cairns is the northern end of the east coast Australian rail, road, sea and air transport systems. The city was established purely on possibilities as a port, with nothing else to recommend it as site for a city. *Trinity Bay,* around which the city focuses, was named by Captain Cook on Trinity Sunday 1770. The area attracted interest 100 years later when gold was discovered 200 miles away in 1873 on Palmer River, and in 1876 on Hodgkinson River. Although no way was ever managed through the mangroves and swamps from from Trinity Bay to the gold fields, government officials decided Cairns and Trinity Bay would make a good harbor. The town was officially established in 1876, and was named after the governor of Queensland.

The regional population in the Far North Queensland area service by Cairns is about 150,000, having grown rapidly during the 1970's and early 1980's. It is considered somewhat maverick in Australian political circles,voting more conservative (Liberal and National Parties rather than Labor) in the last elections than other parts of the country. This may be partly attributed to shifting government attitudes about supporting the sugar cane industry, upon which a good part of the state depends.

Cairns' current population is over 50,000, and it is often described as *the mecca for big game fishermen from all over Australia and overseas.* Fishing season is in the spring out of Cairns (September through December), and its claims to be the best big game fishing place in the world could well be valid. Catches include tuna, barracuda, sailfish, shark, and black marlin, the biggest and fiercest of all game fish. Cairns is the *black marlin* capital of the world. From the Marlin Jetty along Cairns' Esplanade, you can watch the marlin being weighed-in.

Getting from the airport to town is a snap.There are several taxis, and you will also find a friendly limousine service, which will take you directly to your hotel or where ever else in town you want to be dropped off for $A3 per person.

Hotels, or chiefly, motels, in and around the town are abundant. The modern *Pacific International* with twelve floors, easily dominates the local skyline, and is located on the Esplanade within sight of the wharf and all of the charter and sight seeing boat services. It is also a block from the main down town area, and within easy walking distance of airline offices, banks and stores. Rooms are air conditioned and pleasantly appointed, with color television and international direct dial telephones, and the views of the harbor or the coast are both excellent.

Naturally, the first thing to do after arriving in town is to walk around and get your bearings. If you arrive at lunch time, as we did, and if you get hungry while walking along the Marlin Jetty and the Esplanade, *Tawny's* serves an excellent fresh fish lunch and is *fully licensed* (meaning the full range of refreshments are available without having to bring your own). The baramundi and wrass were both excellent, and the wine list offered a fine broad selection of Australian wines.

The other leading fresh fish restaurant nearby is the *Waterfront Restaurant* in the *Pacific International Hotel*. Their presentation of Queensland mud crab was outstanding. People in town may recommend that you try *Barnacle Bill's,* also on the Esplanade, a block further past the *Pacific International*. Bill's was popular the evening we were there, but we concluded it was not due to the cuisine.

The town is dotted with small restaurants of a variety of nationalities and offerings –pizza, Chinese, Mexican,Indonesian, local – some licensed, to serve alcoholic beverages, but most not. Seafood and tropical fruits are restaurant specialties. Local beef, raised just down the Queensland coast, is highly regarded. There are many long-established Chinese restaurants. The abundance of public bars and bottle shops guarantees that one need not do without refreshment.

If you are interested, while you are walking along the wharf, you may want to visit *Reef World,* with live crocodiles on display. If you are not planning to do any snorkeling or scuba diving in the Reef region, you may be attracted to *Windows On The Reef*, also situated nearby on the waterfront, a floating deck using special effects to give the impression of *diving* 100 feet below surface.

Cairns

THE GREAT BARRIER REEF

Downtown Cairns bills itself as a shopping stopover with boutiques and chain stores. Actually, there is an abundance of fairly typical tourism shops selling a variety of teeshirts, opal and coral jewelry and fairly typical Australian souvenirs. If you are interested in purchasing Australian opals, consider buying unset stones to have mounted in the United States. Australian jewelers, even in finer locations in Sydney, commonly use 10 carat settings, which are not often to American taste. Scattered around Abbott Street and the cross streets are the stores and shops typically found in Australian cities – clothing stores, pharmacies, film and camera stores, small restaurants, bottle shops, and the like, making for a pleasant hour stroll around the town.

The nearby town of Kuranda can be reached by a trip aboard the restored railroad or half-hour drive from Cairns along fairly good road. The *Kuranda Scenic Rail* rises 1000 feet in thirteen miles, passing through fifteen tunnels and a mile of bridges, some over ravines hundreds of feet deep. From Cairns the rail trip is one and a half hours in each direction.

There are a few car rental agencies in Cairns, listed under *motor car hire* in the yellow pages, or available through your hotel. Do remember to drive **left** in Australia. Your U.S. or Canadian driver's license is accepted. If you plan to be there at a busy time of year, you had better reserve your car in advance through Hertz, Avis or one of the other international companies which will accept reservations.Incidentally, most rental companies are very cooperative about having you leave your car at the Cairns airport at no additional charge, and drop-off charges generally are waived or nominal between major points. If you are leaving Cairns via a domestic air carrier, the counter agents will accept your contract and car keys, if there is no car drop off office in the particular departure area.

If you do drive to Kuranda, the turnoff from Captain Cook Highway to Kuranda is not clearly marked. We were fortunate that someone had etched *Kuranda* in the dust of the road sign. In case it has rained since we visited, however, turn left at the sign to Mareeba, shortly after you have passed the Cairns airport general aviation terminal, which is on your right.

Kuranda's main industry today is tourism. Because of its altitude, the town is *naturally air-conditioned*. Just outside of town, or as part of your train ride, you will see *Barron Falls* and *Barron Gorge*. You can take a *Barron River Cruise* aboard the *Kuranda Queen* , departing from the railway station landing daily except Sunday, connecting with all trains. (Sunday hourly departure 10:00 a.m. to 4:00 p.m.)

Army Duck Tours begin at Mountain Groves, which you reach just before entering Kuranda, and take you through rain forest mountains and valleys aboard a six wheel drive amphibian. Tours at 10:00 and 11:30 a.m., and 2:30 p.m. You may enjoy a brief walk through Kuranda, which is now two blocks or so of predominantly souvenir and tourist shops. You can lunch in one of their pubs or small restaurants, and return to Cairns the way you came.

If you are interested in a longer drive and wish to see some of Australia's interesting interior, consider returning to Cairns along a loop that continues past Kuranda, across the Atherton Tableland, and toward Mareeba, and then toward Mossman, and back to the coast. If you are intending to take this drive, however, remember to get a map of the region from your car rental agency and still be prepared to ask the very friendly locals along the way for directions when the road signs leave you a bit mystified.

THE GREAT BARRIER REEF

This three hour drive takes you across the dairy and farmlands of the region, and you can begin to appreciate the huge farms which exist in this land of tremendous open spaces. The crops here include corn and potatoes; some tobacco is grown near Mareeba north of the tableland. There are several tiny towns, but they are many miles apart, as are residences along the way. As you drive, you will probably notice, along the roadside and among the trees, puzzling large mounds of dried earthen clay. These are *giant ant hills* which, until the advent of new synthetic supersurfaces, provided the material for many of Australia's superb clay tennis courts, for which the country enjoyed such fame.

Cairns

The road, except where the Queensland government road crews are busy maintaining and improving, is very good for country driving, but do expect occasional flagmen where there is grading going on or a road has been partially washed out during winter flash flooding. As we indicated, however, road signs are not good. After you have traveled around fifty kilometers almost due west from Kuranda you will reach Mareeba, keeping to the right at the *Y,* just before the town, proceed north about forty kilometers to Mount Molloy. After passing through this tiny town, you will come to a division in the road, where you keep again to the right, following the road to the Captain Cook highway and back toward Cairns.

Upon connecting with the coast highway, you will see signs on the left to *Port Douglas.* This three or four mile detour is well worth a brief visit, unless you are very pressed for time. Formerly an important gold rush town, Port Douglas is now a small lazy coastal resort and fishing village which is as laid back as you will find. If you have not had lunch by the time you get there (and it's before 2:00 p.m. when all the local restaurants stop serving) try the *Courthouse Hotel.* You make your selection from a blackboard featuring a good choice of grilled dishes, and then walk back to the kitchen to place your order. On your way to or from the kitchen, stop at the pub and order your beer or wine to go with the lunch.

The drive from Port Douglas back to Cairns is about forty-five miles (75 kilometers or so on your Australian odometer). It is a very pleasant and picturesque trip along the coast, passing many of Cairns better beaches, which are found to the north of the city. Should this be your day of departure from Cairns, you will arrive at the airport saving yourself a few miles on the return journey along this same road, and you can drop your rental car there at the airport.

Townsville

Named for Robert Towns, who in 1864 reluctantly decided to approve the site as the rendering works to serve nearby cattle stations, the city originally grew on the strength of the gold rush. Chosen in the late 1950's as the site for a bulk sugar terminal, now new glass and concrete towers dot the city. The most obvious of these is the *sugar shaker* – a cylindrical downtown highrise building housing the *International Hotel,* restaurant, and TAA offices among others. Townsville, Australia's largest tropical city, is the second largest in Queensland (next to Brisbane) with a current population over 100,000, and if the state ever is split in two, it is likely this will be capital of Northern Queensland state.

Shopping plazas and malls – particular the new *Flinders Mall* – give the central business district a very modern look, although there are interesting examples of turn-of-the century commercial architecture standing side by side with the new shops. This international air gateway to the Great Barrier Reef (it continues to handle flights from Asia, particularly Singapore, and some from Europe and North America, although Cairns is slated to get most of the direct U.S. traffic) is a center of North Queensland commercial development and scientific research. *Captain Cook University* and the headquarters of the *Great Barrier Reef Marine Park Authority* are situated here.

The artificial harbor out of Ross Creek is excellent for both large and small boats. From the harbor there is a fine view of Magnetic Island which dominates the skyline five miles across Cleveland Bay. Here Hayle's ferry leaves regularly for the island with ten ferries daily for the forty minute trip. Townsville is the base for day cruises and air tours to that island as well as for day and overnight trips to the Outer Reef.

THE GREAT BARRIER REEF

The best accommodations in town are in the *sugar shaker*, the modern *Townsville International Hotel*. Rooms have good views of the city and of Cleveland Bay, balconies, refrigerator, coffee and tea maker, color TV with in-house movies, and direct dial telephones. In the downtown area, there is also *Lowths Hotel,* and near the beach are the *Bessell Lodge International Motel* and the *Townsville Travelodge,* both with good views and facilities.

The Reef Link ($A60 per person, drinks extra) leaves from the Flinders Street terminal opposite the Greyhound Bus terminal at 9:30 a.m. and returns at 5:00. It carriers 144 passengers aboard

a 70' catama ran over the 38 miles to the Outer Reef at 30 knots in just about 80 minutes. There, passengers transfer to floating pontoons which serve as a base from which guests can swim, snorkel and dive. There is also a helipad. After a smorgasbord lunch, passengers board the Yellow Sub which slowly moves across the John Brewer Reef for a forty-five minute ride, during which fish which are viewed from the sub-sea fisheye glass windows are hand fed.

Airlie Beach and **Shute Harbor** (population 1710).

Shute Harbor is the launch departure point for the Whitsunday Group of islands, and Airlie Beach (about seven miles away) is the tourist resort, service center and dormitory for visitors to the area. Neither boasts a good beach. Whitsunday Field, the home base of Air Whitsunday, is situated about midway between Shute Harbor and Airlie Beach. Buses,and a very occasional taxi ,connect the two communities, as well as linking them with the airport serving Proserpine a few miles away.

Huge catamaran ferries call at Shute Harbor serving Telford South Molle, Hamilton, and Hayman resorts, and there is a water taxi serving Whitsunday 100 just across the bay on Long Island. Launches take passengers from here to the other Whitsunday Passage resorts and islands. Many day trips of the region are based here. Two of the major boat charter companies (*Whitsunday Rent-a-Yacht* and *Australian Bare Boat* Charter) are also situated in Shute Harbor.

This good-sized harbor is very well protected by surrounding hills against almost all of the weather experienced in the region, and offers many moorings and ample space for anchorages. It is also a fairly convenient overnight harbor for bareboats and charters cruising the Whitsundays, so there are usually many boats moored in the bay on an average evening. Fresh water is available at the harbor for yachts, and there is a small souvenir and sundries shop, as well as an adjoining coffee shop. There are, however, no other tourist facilities such as restaurants or hotels.

Airlie Beach, five miles north, has grown from a sleepy village a few years ago to a bustling resort town. There are already many motels, lots of campgrounds and *caravans* (trailer parks) as well as several substantial resorts including **The Terraces**, and **Whitsunday Village. Wanderers Paradise**, Melanesian family-style units with refrigerator, stove, crockery, laundry facilities, nightly entertainment, swimming pools, and tennis courts, was formerly owned by TransAustralia Airlines, which recently sold the resort. However, the best hotel in town is probably the **Coral Sea Resort** with similar facilities.

There is a post office, many souvenir and T-shirt shops, and the news agency (mid-way along the town's main street on the west side) with an excellent selection of books on Australia, yachting, fishing, as well as general reading material. There is a TAA reservations office and several travel and sightseeing booking agencies, a medical office, two firms of solicitors (lawyers, that is, one of which you will need should you wish to acquire or convey property here), a small super market, yacht sales and rental offices, and Avis and Budget car rental agencies, among other businesses.

For a town of this size, Airlie Beach has an exceptional supply of good restaurants. *Romeo's,* set back from the east side of the street between a travel agency and a hair salon, is an outstanding Italian restaurant which could hold its own, indeed excel, in almost any American city. The restaurant is right on the beach, and there is seating on the beach veranda, inside, or in a pleasant front courtyard. Service was very attentive, and the owner personally supervises both the open kitchen and the dining room.

Romeo's fresh pasta was absolutely superb. The fresh fish was even more outstanding, particularly the succulent barbecued Moreton Bay bugs (those miniature lobsters from South Queensland, served about six to a portion, covered with garlic butter). Romeo himself is a transplanted Melbournean who refused all our blandishments and cajolery to get him to relocate in the United States. If this restaurant is closed or too busy, your next best bet is to try *Moon's* at the south end of town for fresh seafood or the fine restaurant at the **Coral Sea Resort.**

CARDWELL

West of Rockingham Bay, protected by the heights of Hinchinbrook Island, Cardwell is a center of a major national park area and is near Australia's *Bananaland.* It is a small resort town with no anchorage, so small boats use new the concrete wharf. Here you can rent boats and yachts for plying the Hinchinbrook Channel and may also take sailing lessons if you wish.

COOKTOWN

This is the most northern center of population on the eastern coast, and it is about as far as you can go by road without special equipment. Cook's ship, the *Endeavor,* found shelter here. About this near-ghost town (population 920), full of character, the Australian Tourist Commission says, *Some 80 years ago gold brought overnight prosperity to Cooktown.The ghosts of times past are the few remaining great solid banks which face a main street of gentle grass and lush trees.* This was the first place a kangaroo was ever seen by a European – Cook's party. One hundred years later it became the center of Australia's northern gold rush, and when the rush petered out, Cooktown's boom economy collapsed.

koala   bears

INGHAM

A flourishing sugar cane city adjacent to the Hinchinbrook Channel, with two mills, Ingham has a diverse ethnic population including residents of Italian, Basque, Spanish and Flemish extraction.

INISFAIL

Thought by some to be the prettiest town on the coast and, because of its position next to the mountains, one of the wettest towns on the entire continent. It is surrounded by heavy tropical growth because of the Johnstone and South Johnstone Rivers on its doorsteps. It was a center for *blackbirding,* the nineteenth century trade in Pacific islands slaves, for cane work in the lush fields surrounding the town. After the Palmer River gold supply dwindled, many Chinese drifted to Inisfail; later many Italian laborers were brought in. During World War II many of the Italians were interned, but since then the town has become a harmonious multi-ethnic community.

LUCINDA

On Hinchinbrook Channel, this is a facility for large ships to load cane sugar and molasses. The bulk sugar wharf is probably the longest of its type in the world, an amazing 3-mile long slender wharf completed in 1979, permitting ships to load and unload without having to enter the Hinchinbrook Channel.

MACKAY (population 40,000)

A business and tourist city, surrounded by tropical palms and parks. Sugarcane is the main industry. Its large artificial harbor hosts the world's largest sugar terminal, and also a large coal handling complex.

THE GREAT BARRIER REEF

MISSION BEACH and TULLY

These are the main local access points to Dunk Island. Locals refer to this as the *real tropics*. Separated from Bruce Highway by rain forest, this is one of the only areas of lowland rain forest left in the tropics and is the only surviving remnant at sea level. Known as *Complex Mesophyl Lowland Vineforest*, you can see ferns, vines, orchids, wild banana, and wild ginger. The forest is inhabited by cassowary (a large flightless bird slightly smaller than the emu or the ostrich), scrubfowl, parrots, wallaby and numerous varieties of large tropical butterflies. There are nearby banana, pineapple and paw paw (papaya) plantations, and a Sunday morning market at *Wongaling Corner*. **The Mission Beach Resort** is situated in the rain forest close to the beach. It features air conditioned rooms with radio, color television, telephones, tea and coffee maker. There is a pool and well marked walking tracks through the forest.

Nearby Tully is a center of the sugar growing district producing one million tons of cane per year. It is also known for bananas and other tropical fruits as well as for cattle ranching. *King Ranch*, the well known American concern, has developed area covering approximately 50,000 acres to the west. Tully has the highest average annual rainfall (170 inches) of any town in Australia.

ROCKHAMPTON

Rockhampton (population 50,000) is a provincial city on the banks of the Fitzroy River, which can be brown and muddy and not terribly attractive. The town looks much like a small U.S. town circa 1945. This area is famous for beef cattle, and is also a sugar cane center.*Quay Street* in the city, one block from the main downtown shopping street, is intact from its 19th century beginnings, but little has been done to make the street or the town particularly attractive to tourists. *Rocky* is the access point for Great Keppel Island and is not really worth a special visit. If you have time between planes or whatever, try the *Heritage Tavern* on Quay Street for an ample, inexpensive, and quite pleasant lunch.

Cairns

Lizard Island

MORE
INTERESTING
THINGS

In this chapter we pass along information about a few additional ideas for vacation activities, a word about departure formalities, and some potential useful sources of additional information.

SIGHTSAILING and FLIGHTSEEING

Sailing or flying to the Outer Barrier Reef, or around groups of islands, is an easy and reasonably economical way of exploring areas of the Great Barrier Reef and its cays, atolls and islands. The *M.V. Quicksilver,* a high speed catamaran with bar, sundeck, fresh-water shower and swimming platform, operated by the same people who run the day trip to the Low Islets, leaves Port Douglas wharf daily at 10:30 a.m. for a 90 minute trip to St. Crispin Reef on the Outer Barrier Reef ($A49, drinks extra; $A55 includes round trip bus connection from Cairns). There, in the Coral Sea, you can swim, snorkel, explore via glass bottom boat and scuba dive (they will rent you equipment if you hold a certificate from a recognized dive organization). The cruise includes smorgasbord lunch, including fresh-water prawns; a video film about the Great Barrier Reef, and free use of equipment (except scuba gear and underwater cameras, which must be rented). The *Quicksilver* returns to Port Douglas at 4:30 p.m.

The Coral Reefel is a floating 82' long by 30' wide hotel moored at Michaelmas Cay on the Outer Barrier Reef. Reached aboard the *Supa Cat* from Cairns, after a 2 1/2 hour stop at Green Island, guests arrive at the hotel around noon. Very basic accommodations are in twin bed, air-conditioned cabins. There is a small lounge bar with TV. Activities include bird watching, snorkeling (underwater cameras are available on request), glass bottom boat, and sport fishing (by arrangement).

There are day charters for game and marlin fishing from Cairns, as well as several other island visit cruises. The reservations office is situated right on the wharf on the Esplanade. There are also numerous extended cruises (up to a 14 day cruise aboard *M.V. Auriga Bay* to Thursday Island at the northeast tip of Australia) which can be booked from Cairns. Similarly, from Townsville, there are numerous one- and multi-day cruises to nearby islands and to the Outer Reef.

From Mackay Roylen Cruises operates five-day cruises aboard the 114' *M.V. Roylen Endeavor* , carrying 45 passengers in air conditioned cabins throughout the year ($A645 per person, double bed suite, meals included; $A557, cabins with private baths; $466, cabins with shared facilities). These trips call at the Great Barrier Reef (weather permitting), the Whitsunday Islands and Brampton Island. A similar cruise from Mackay is operated by *Elizabeth E Coral Cruises* aboard its 112' vessel ($A445, meals included).

Air Whitsunday (P.O. Box 166, Airlie Beach, Qld. 4802;

telephone: [79] 469 133) offers several *Reef Adventures.* There are many brief sightseeing flights ($A20-75, depending upon length) over the Outer Reef. On Wednesdays they will fly you to the 112' T.S.M.V. *Reef Encounter Sandra,* moored at the Outer Reef for a full day at Hardy Reef ($A115 inclusive, without scuba gear), departing Whitsunday Field at 8:00 a.m. The day is spent reef walking, snorkeling, coral viewing on a glass bottomed boat, scuba diving (if you are qualified), or fishing, with lunch included. For longer stays, the *Reef Encounter,* with crew of 9, including PADI dive instructor

and marine biologist, has twin cabin accommodations for a maximum of 25 guests. ($A490, 7 days, inclusive except scuba; $A440 5 days; $A245 two days; $A165 Saturday a.m. to Sunday p.m.; $158 overnight.)

In addition, Air Whitsunday offers *scuba diving packages* at the Reef Encounter from 2 days ($A305) to 7 days ($640), with an introductory shallow water training and single-dive *resort course* ($A45) and additional instructed dives ($A30 first dive, $A20 second dive, including all gear and an instructor buddy). All necessary scuba gear can be rented, including regulators and even (by arrangement 24 hours prior to the flight) underwater Nikonos cameras and strobes.

For their piece de resistance Air Whitsunday offers a Great Barrier *Flying Boat Cruise* ($A1870 per person, twin accommodations, inclusive) which departs either Cairns or Brisbane and includes visits to Dunk, Hinchinbrook and Orpheus Islands, Brewer Reef and the Yellow Sub, Hardy Lagoon, the Reef Encounter, Great Keppel Island, Lady Musgrave Island and Fraser Island. This one excursion, operated in the tradition of Flying Boat Style, incorporates a broad cross-section of Great Barrier Reef activities and some of its finest attractions.

Further information regarding Air Whitsunday may also be obtained through SO/PA, 1448 15th Street, Suite 105, Santa Monica, California 90404; telephone [213] 393-8262 or [800] 472-5-15, or Maritime World, 2618 Newport Blvd., Newport Beach,California 92663; telephone [714] 675-2250, reservations collect.

BAREBOAT CHARTERS in the Whitsunday

An increasingly popular way to see the Whitsunday Group of islands is by *chartering a yacht or motor cruiser* from one of the many charter companies operating on the coast or Hamilton Island. Currently, there are accommodations for over four hundred people available on charter boats in this region, and many people are using this method to see several resort and uninhabited islands without restricting themselves to a single hotel. Charters are possible with or without crew, and on boats of a wide variety of sizes and shapes.

Australian Bareboat Charters (P.O.Box 115, Airlie Beach, Qld. 4802; telephone [79] 469 381) includes in its fleet yachts from 25' to 47' and 36' motor cruisers. They also book the 75' crewed *Pegasus* which accommodates 8 very comfortably. **Whitsunday Rent-a-Yacht** (Shute Harbor), 4802, Qld; telephone [79] 469 232) has yachts ranging from 22' to 60' and 34' motor cruisers. **Mandalay Sailing** (P.O. Box 218, Airlie Beach, Qld. 4802; telephone [79] 466 298), which operates it own marina outside of Airlie Beach, rents yachts from 25' to 50' and 30' and 34' motor cruisers. Hamilton Island also has charter yacht services. Weekly bare boat rates (that is, without crew or provisions) run from $A750-2500 depending upon length and capacity, with some boats having four berths and others six or eight. Provisions will run $A15-20 per day per person additional. Crew is $A70-100 extra, per crew member.

Boats are usually fully equipped with dinghies and outboards, bed linens, kitchen equipment, short wave radio, and fishing gear. All of the charter operators will be pleased to send you current brochures with prices and schematic drawings of the boats showing facilities and accommodations. One bit of advice: unless you really enjoy tightly compacted crowds, discount the charterer's estimate of comfortable accommodations by 25-50% in deciding how many to include in your group, particularly if you are planning more than a few days aboard.

Additional information regarding charters may be obtained from Yachting World Yacht Charters, 680 Beach Street, Suite 498, San Francisco, California 94109; telephone [415] 928-4480 or [800] 227-5436, or SO/PAC, 1448 15th Street, Suite 105, Santa Monica, California 90404; telephone [213] 393-8262 or [800] 472-5051

DEPARTURE FORMALITIES

Australia exacts a departure tax for every person 12 years of age and over,of $A20 before leaving Australia, to be paid at special windows at international airports. A stamp indicating that the tax has been paid is affixed to your plane tickets, so you should allow time for taking care of this before you check in for your flight. Formerly, stamps could be purchased in Australian currency only, but now the tax stamp offices will accept all major credit cards.

MORE INFORMATION

There are several excellent sources of information fairly easily available to American tourists, which will give you current prices, resort sizes, telephone numbers and the like.

MORE INTERESTING THINGS

The first thing you probably should do when you are ready to plan your trip is to contact the **Australian Tourist Commission**, 3550 Wilshire Blvd., Suite 1740, Los Angeles, CA 90010; telephone: [213] 380-6060, or Suite 2908, 1270 Avenue of the Americas, New York, NY 10020; telephone: [212] 489-7550 or [800] 445-4400. Ask them to send you the latest editions of any of their publications, as well as any information they may be able to send regarding islands in which you are interested.

The international air carriers can provide you with unlimited information about Great Barrier Reef vacations. Both of Australia's domestic carriers maintain offices in North America, and reservations and travel arrangements can be made through them.

Ansett Airlines of Australia
5000 Birch Street
Suite 3000 West Tower
Newport Beach, CA 92660
[714] 476-0892
[800] 626-7388 in California
[800] 426-7388 outside of California

TransAustralia Airlines
230 Park Avenue, Suite 921/922
New York, NY 10969
Information: [212] 986-3772
Reservations: [800] 472-5015

510 West Sixth Street
Los Angeles, CA 90014
Information and *reservations:* [213] 626-2352

THE GREAT BARRIER REEF

225 North Michigan Avenue
Chicago, IL 60601
Information: [312] 565-0803
Reservation: [800] 472-5015

For further information regarding any of the island resorts, and particularly as to making reservations for any that do not have U.S. booking agents, contact the **Queensland Tourist and Travel Corp.**, 3550 Wilshire Boulevard, Suite 1738, Los Angeles, California 90010; telephone [213] 381-3062.

The Reef

Without doubt Australia's Great Barrier Reef offers a unique variety of tropical vacation experiences. From intimate to large, low to mountainous, informal to elegant, this collection of resorts has it all. This exciting venue is offered on a series of refreshingly uncrowded islands, where a thousand people (as on Hamilton) is a veritable metropolis, while a guest population of sixty or less (perhaps Lizard, Orpheus or Hinchinbrook) is not at all out of the ordinary. Set all this down in one of the world's truly spectacular natural structures and you have the makings for many memorable journeys.

Day by day the area is becoming more popular. Australians are discovering their national treasure, and Americans are not far behind. Resorts are expanding (fortunately at a modest rate by U.S. standards), although the government is committed to the proposition that remaining uninhabited islands will stay undeveloped.

But change here is, as everywhere, inevitable. During the six months between two of our visits, the major regional airline was acquired by the government owned national carrier, a new resort's central complex burned to the ground, another resort announced a complete cessation of operations for nine months during major remodeling, another old line family resort sold to a national airline, two resorts doubled their capacity (from thirty to a mere sixty guests on an entire island), and another announced plans to move the resort from one side of the tiny island to the other.

Fortunately, here change is almost always modest and moderate. With but one resort facility to most of these islands, growth still means you will always be able to find a private spot on a quiet beach for a lovely picnic, sail in uncrowded waters or snorkel in beautiful tropical lagoons, finding privacy or activity as you desire.

By the time you visit the area, the 200 room floating Reeftel out of Townsville on the Barrier Reef itself will be operational. Elsewhere there undoubtedly will be more and more sub-mersibles (these remarkable new power barges that cruise around on the surface of the lagoons with their huge under-water windows) visiting the reef, more flights to and around the area, more boats for hire, more hotel rooms, all the while preserving vast open spaces, uncrowded beaches, dense forests, friendly resorts.

Arne and Ruth Werchick

We hope that your travels to this remarkable region are as filled with pleasure as ours have been. We would be indebted to those of you who could find the time to share your Great Barrier Reef experiences with us. A postcard from your favorite island, a note to keep us abreast of changes, even a memo setting right anything you think needs correcting, will be much appreciated. Send your comments to us

Arne and Ruth Werchick

to let us know what's happening in our favorite corner of the world. And give a scrap of your breakfast toast to a friendly wallaby or a passing parrot fish for us.